THE HOWS AND WHYS OF ALTERNATIVE EDUCATION

Schools Where Students Thrive

Darlene Leiding

Rowman & Littlefield Education
Lanham, Maryland • Toronto • Plymouth, UK
2008

Published in the United States of America
by Rowman & Littlefield Education
A Division of Rowman & Littlefield Publishers, Inc.
A wholly owned subsidiary of
The Rowman & Littlefield Publishing Group, Inc.
4501 Forbes Boulevard, Suite 200, Lanham, Maryland 20706
www.rowmaneducation.com

Estover Road
Plymouth PL6 7PY
United Kingdom

British Library Cataloguing in Publication Information Available

Library of Congress Cataloging-in-Publication Data

Leiding, Darlene, 1943–
The hows and whys of alternative education : schools where students thrive / Darlene Leiding.
p. cm.
Includes bibliographical references.
ISBN-13: 978-1-57886-687-8 (hardback : alk. paper)
ISBN-10: 1-57886-687-1 (hardback : alk. paper)
ISBN-13: 978-1-57886-688-5 (pbk. : alk. paper)
ISBN-10: 1-57886-688-X (pbk. : alk. paper)
1. Alternative schools—United States. 2. Alternative education—United States. 3. Educational change—United States. I. Title.
LC46.4.L45 2008
371.040973—dc22
2007025345

∞™ The paper used in this publication meets the minimum requirements of American National Standard for Information Sciences—Permanence of Paper for Printed Library Materials, ANSI/NISO Z39.48-1992.
Manufactured in the United States of America.

CONTENTS

INTRODUCTION

> To each of us, at certain points of our lives, there come opportunities to rearrange our formulas and assumptions not necessarily to be rid of the old, but more to profit from adding something new.
>
> —Leo Buscaglia

I am 16. My high school is a big crowded building. I have to stay inside until I can earn "off-campus privileges." Since I am a kid, the adults expect that I'll cut corners. "Do you have a hall pass, kid?" I hate security guards.

My classes are 47 minutes long. I go to seven in a row with 20 minutes out for lunch. I don't talk much in my classes because mostly the teachers want me to listen. Teachers don't have the time to get to know me. My guidance counselor hustles me out of her office when I want to talk, reminding me that she has 249 other kids to counsel.

Even though I get "promoted" every year no one really knows what I learned last year or what exactly I still need to learn. That's because the curriculum changes all the time, and because my teachers never seem to talk about me with each other.

We take a lot of standardized tests, but they're not very hard. We spend lots of class time learning how to outsmart multiple-choice questions and fill in bubble sheets. As though that's what life is all about. What a joke!

I come to school because I can hang out with my homies. The teachers dumb down the material to make it easy because I am "inner city black." I'm scared about my future. I'm not learning much that I can use to get a job. My God, what lies ahead?

Over the last 3 decades, many have dolefully described the American school and its anonymity and inefficiencies, but few have made sustained efforts to change it. This is no surprise as schools are complicated places where everything important connects with everything else and many long-established practices, of whatever educational merit, have powerful symbolic value. One messes with these at one's peril.

Isn't it interesting that from birth through toddlerhood, children don't have teachers, except for their parents, books, or preconceived objectives as to when and what they must learn by a certain time. Yet, amazingly, they do learn, developing by leaps and bounds. What causes this to happen? How can babies learn without someone dictating to them what they must know? Left to their own means, a baby learns through desire, environment, modeling, exploring, experimentation, repetition, and encouragement. In 3 years they go from helpless to an independent, capable being who is thrown into the "lion's den" known as "school." From here on in, children will be told, monitored, commanded, permitted, molded, "graded," tested, and made to feel inadequate if they can't achieve something by a certain time, in the name of education. Forget what the child is interested in, forget an enticing, friendly atmosphere, forget monitoring as opposed to directing, forget the joy of self-discovery and trial and error, and forget people who cheer the child on in spite of adversity. No, now children will become pigeonholed, stifled, and automated, the fine product of their systematic education.

Sadly, many children become lost in this institutionalized environment and ideology. They lose interest in learning and, most of all, belief in their ability. They want to be more in control of their own destiny. They have strengths that cause them to be excited, but they have weaknesses that cause them to avoid or shut down. They need a balance of areas where they can thrive, with smaller portions, patience, and more time to develop strengths. Above all, they need adults who mentor and encourage instead of ones who determine they are bad in math or reading and cast them aside or worse, give up on them in favor of the more "gifted" in that area. Children always need to feel that they count no matter what their ability. They need the developmental freedom they had as babies.

Thankfully, alternative schools are trying to do just this, bringing back the joy and freedom of learning. Though each school is different in its focus and means, alternative schools, schools of choice if you will, want to help children gain back their autonomy in education. They are trying to allow desire to be more the determiner of subjects. They are trying to create smaller, more positive, and less institutionalized learning environments where kids feel more comfortable and will want to come to school. These schools encourage students to seek role models and community leaders to help them find out more about an area than just the teachers hired by the school can. Not only does this help students get different perspectives, ideas, and overall instruction, but it also allows them to discover the world is the school, not the building. In schools of choice, students are given the freedom to experiment and explore and to find out more about their area of interest and also about themselves. They are encouraged to think outside the box and run in whatever direction the ideas lead. The teachers at these schools are prompted to take an interest in what the child is interested in rather than judging if something is worthwhile or not. Student-teacher ratios are lower so teachers are more available to the students, and the structure is less formal. Students feel more comfortable seeking out the assistance of the teacher. In other words, these schools are seeking to provide children a place where they will want to learn, not have to learn.

An agenda item promoted by the government is the No Child Left Behind Act. At face value, it is very commendable and should be an educational mantra. It is, however, not devoted to helping students learn, but having them score properly on tests. The reality is, all children want to and can learn anything. What the "system" has lost sight of is what it takes to do so. Hopefully, alternative programs will forge ahead and become an example of nurturing the joy of learning that seems to be absent in our schools today.

From the president of the United States to the president of the local parent-teacher association, everyone is talking about schools. More than ever before people recognize the value of quality education for all students. The demand for well-educated, highly skilled workers is growing. Education provides more than job skills. It teaches self-discipline, creativity, and patience. It prepares people to cope with change.

Because Americans have so many different expectations for education, it is difficult to determine just how well schools are doing today. Schools that successfully educate children come in a variety of sizes and styles. Some cater to only the most motivated children, others attempt to educate all who come through their doors. Some have adequate funding, well-equipped facilities, and the best teachers. Others make do with less and still provide an excellent education.

One example of a successful, innovative school is Thayer Junior/Senior High Academy located in the small town of Winchester, New Hampshire. Thayer is different from most public schools in that schedules are relaxed, no bells ring at the end of each hour, and classes are informal. Sofas, rocking chairs, and tables replace traditional desks. Teachers help students to think creatively, to become independent learners, and to care for each other. Projects are practical and varied, and students must demonstrate certain learning skills and basic academic knowledge before they can graduate. Life after Thayer classes are mandatory to give seniors information about careers, advice on handling social issues, and lessons in life skills such as apartment hunting and budgeting. As one teacher said, "kids leave here with a better sense of who they are, how they fit into society, what their options are, and what they can be."

Located several hundred miles south of Thayer is another example of a successful public alternative school. Malcolm X Elementary Charter School is located in one of the toughest neighborhoods in Washington, D.C. This school appears to succeed against all odds. Outside, sirens and gunfire are common. Inside, the staff combines encouragement, high expectations, and firm discipline to provide inspiration and a safe environment for students. Everyone from the principal to the security guard works together to convince at-risk children that education is their ticket to a better life. Test scores are not as high as those of well-to-do suburban children, but attendance at Malcolm X is at 93%. Parents volunteer their time, monitor their child's homework, and make sure they are in school. One parent reported, "I can honestly say my daughter will have a great future." Another parent adds, "This school is a school that you can be proud to send your child to."

Education is the great equalizer in American society. It unlocks the doors to children's futures. It's the key to accessing opportunity and getting ahead in this country. Of course, education isn't a surefire guarantee of success in life, but statistics show beyond a shadow of a doubt that the better educated you are, the better you will be economically. Getting a good education has always given one a good leg up in life. That was true in days gone by, and it is truer today than ever before. The main reason is the way the U.S. labor market has changed over the years.

During the 1950s, just about 80% of all the jobs in the economy were semiskilled or unskilled. That means most workers years ago didn't require much in the way of formal education. Even if they never finished high school, they could easily earn enough, for instance, as factory workers to enjoy a decent standard of living, buy a home, a car, take an occasional vacation, and send their kids off to college. The exact opposite is true today. Eighty-five percent of all jobs today are skilled or professional. The bottom line is that you need a solid education in order to succeed in the information-age economy of the 21st century.

The sad fact is that there is a crisis in our classrooms. In virtually every school district across America, many students achieve at lower levels, earn lousier test scores, are placed more frequently into special education or remedial and less challenging classes, and are discouraged from striving to excel academically, or from demanding excellence from themselves. The perception is that they are intellectually inferior. A perception which many educators in our schools tragically reinforce.

Students who can barely read by the fourth grade face a steep uphill climb the rest of the way through school and later in life. They will struggle with the reading assignments in social studies, the writing assignments in English class, and the word problems in math. They may not be able to pass the tough exams that states are imposing for moving from grade to grade and for graduating from high school. Higher education will be off limits. The good jobs that provide for the good life will be out of reach for young people who are not prepared academically.

In 1983 the U.S. Department of Education released the report *A Nation at Risk*, which proclaimed that the quality of public education had deteriorated since the 1950s. The average scholastic aptitude test (SAT) scores of college-bound seniors had fallen 16 points, students were scoring much lower on standardized tests than their counterparts in other industrialized countries, and the dropout rate had risen.

In April 1998, a group of educators, policy makers, and business leaders representing various points on the political spectrum gathered at a conference sponsored by the Heritage Foundation and several other organizations to discuss what had happened with American education since *A Nation at Risk* was published. The conclusions were announced in an educational reform manifesto titled "A Nation Still at Risk," published in the July/August 1998 issue of *Policy Review*.

According to "A Nation Still at Risk," the quality of public education in the United States remains below standard. Americans appear to have become complacent about educational issues. Meanwhile, American students remain unprepared for college and for the workforce. Since 1983, more than 10 million students have reached their senior year in high school with no basic reading skills, and 20 million have been promoted to the12th grade without having learned math fundamentals. During this same period, more than 6 million students dropped out of school, a number that includes 30% to 40% of school-age American Indian, African American, and first generation Hispanic students (Williams, 2004, p.12).

"A Nation Still at Risk" goes on to say that the average SAT score in 1998 showed a drop of 55 points on the verbal section and 23 points on the math (p.16). According to another standardized test conducted by the National Assessment of Educational Progress, half of all 17-year-old students cannot calculate the area of a rectangle, and only 20% are able to write a one-paragraph letter to apply for a job. It gets worse . . . 33% thought Columbus reached the New World after 1750, 62% were unable to place the Civil War in the years between 1850 and 1900, 33% did not know what *Brown v. Board of Education* changed, 47% could not express the fraction 9/100 as a percent, 33% did not know where the Mississippi River is located or that it flows to the Gulf of Mexico, and so forth (p.19).

Parents, educators, and policy makers have responded by pushing for reform. Many have called for the use of state-funded tuition vouchers; the development of charter schools, magnet schools, or alternative schools; and allowing low-income parents to use state funds to send their children to high-quality private schools.

In this global age of information, nothing should alarm American parents and leaders more than the failure of our public schools. As quality education of the young becomes the true international currency, that commodity, unfortunately, is in short supply. American schoolchildren, as stated above, lag far behind students in most of the developed world, scoring 19th out of 21 countries in the 2003 Third International Math and Science competition. On domestic exams almost 40% are reading at "below basic" levels.

The quality of public education has declined. On top of this, American students have been encouraged by their baby-boomer teachers to believe that education has to be "fun." Consequently, the resistance to any learning that might seem dry or strenuous has become quite strong. A friend who returned from teaching in Japan said, "Japanese students are more realistic about school. They are socialized to assume that they are in school to learn. They do not expect to have fun or be entertained."

American public education occupies a peculiar position in American life. While all other professions and vocations have advanced in skill and substance, over the last 50 years teaching and learning in grades K–12 has actually regressed. That is, our children are less well educated today than at anytime in history. The situation is particularly unusual because at no time has there been more to learn. Students now too often enter the adult world without the knowledge of an educated person.

What are we doing wrong? We know that children are passionate learners who come into this world with a desire to learn that is as natural as the desire to eat, move, and be loved. Their hunger for knowledge, for skills, for the feeling of mastery is as strong as any other appetite. They learn an amazing variety of things in the years before they enter school, including, miraculously, how to talk fluently in their native language. And they continue learning at a terrifically high rate throughout their childhood.

Then comes the change. We are less likely to see this same passion when we look at kids in school. Something happens to a child when learning is replaced by schooling. Something gets in the way.

I asked a group of third grade students in my school to tell me what they were learning in school. They said, "Don't run in the halls" and "Don't throw stuff." I agreed with them that these were indeed important and showed good behavior. Then I asked them what they felt they needed to learn. There was silence. Finally one girl said, "To listen to the teacher." Another girl said, "To be good." Already, as third graders, learning had become a world of "good children" and "bad children." Good children listen to their teacher. The bad children don't. These children were already becoming disenfranchised as learners and were victims of traditional school culture.

American schools need changing. Everyone seems to agree on this. However, most proposals for educational reform in this country head off in the wrong direction. They change form but not substance. We do not need more hours of school every day or more days of school every year with schools as they now are. We do not need to train students to memorize information just to spit it back on a test. That gives the appearance that students are being educated when they are not. This practice of learning lies at the heart of student boredom and cynicism. Student boredom and cynicism leads to students spending their time and energy on figuring out how to cut classes, cheat, and wiggle out of doing schoolwork. Pretense, boredom, and cynicism are central elements in what is the norm in many American schools today.

Alternative education and schools of choice seem to be able to make a connection between academic pursuit and the world outside for which school is supposed to prepare students. Children deserve to be able to discover the joy and value of growing and learning as a life-long activity for its own sake. Alternative education and the schools mentioned in this book can do all this.

Across the country, parents and students are seeking other options to traditional education. There seems to be an underlying sentiment that traditional schools just don't work for every child. Something has to be done to catch students before they drop out.

Alternative education offers youth who struggle to fit into mainstream schools a viable opportunity for success. For many youth, an alternative school provides a chance to earn school credits, work independently, and hold a job. Alternative education programs can help youth grow emotionally and become more responsible for their behavior.

The rationale for the establishment of most school-choice programs in today's society is that many students require a different type of educational environment and program content in order for them to remain in school, to maximize their full potential as adult citizens, and in some cases, to minimize the adverse effects they may have on other students. Many simply are falling through the cracks and are at risk of not graduating. Our challenge is not to educate the children we want to have, but to educate any child who comes through our school doors. The purpose of schools of choice is to afford students the opportunity to reinforce academic achievement in an environment that is able to fit the individual's needs.

Alternative education offered by schools of choice is a perspective, not a procedure or program. It is based on a belief that there are many ways to become educated, as well as many types of environments and structures within which this may occur. It comes from the recognition that all people can be educated. Therefore, it is a means of incorporating a variety of strategies and choices within the educational system to ensure that every child finds a path to the educational goals of the community.

The school-choice options in the following chapters focus on the academic, emotional/social, and behavioral development of the students served. Expectations are high, but flexible; warm, caring relationships develop; and the curriculum includes individual learning, cooperative learning, team teaching, peer tutoring, and teaching to multiple intelligences. School-linked support services with parents, communities, and social service agencies are important features of these schools. Common elements include a heavy emphasis on the individual, close instructor/student relationships, and relevant hands-on experiential learning. These programs also give a sense of hope and empowerment to students, families, and teachers. Choices are provided which enable each student to succeed. Strengths and values are respected.

Whatever their educational focus or their physical facilities, schools of choice seem to have characteristics that set them apart from their traditional counterparts: smaller units within a larger school, greater ratio of staff to students, individual instruction, noncompetitive environment in which progress is measured by improvement rather than comparison with other students, emphasis on philosophy, instructional methods, school culture, student centered outlooks, and freedom to pursue unconventional methods to achieve educational objectives.

It is true that America has an extensive system of school-choice options, but many say this is both inefficient and discriminates against low-income families and racial minorities.

This book asks the reader to examine our current system and to make sure that a level playing field exists in which schools compete for students, and students and their parents are given the option to exercise their own choices.

A compounding factor is that parents who can afford more expensive homes are much more adept at dealing with the public sector bureaucracies. But what happens to families who cannot afford to buy a house or don't own a car? Are they out of luck? It is almost inevitable that the children of low-income families will end up in schools no one else wants to attend. Does the fault lie with the children? Is the degree of learning taking place due to such outside factors as the students' backgrounds, home life, drugs, alcohol, and genes?

Parents are fighting back. They are turning to homeschooling, charter schools, alternative learning centers, magnet schools, and vouchers for private schools.

Evidence from around the United States supports the contention that allowing parents to choose a child's school improves the child's academic potential and the educational outcomes of students involved. Evidence is also mounting that when the traditional public schools are challenged by the prospect of losing students because of the availability of school choice, the academic performance of both the students who leave and those who remain in the traditional school improves.

I chose to write a book about school choice and will share some thoughts and ideas with you. I have gained much knowledge from colleagues, students, parents, and personal experiences. We are all teachers to one another.

America's educational system is far from perfect. Structural changes are slow in the making. It is kind of like watching a glacier move. In spite of this, dedicated teachers and parents are making a difference.

Change is inevitable; growth is optional. As kids grow up in a rapidly changing society of violence, AIDS, single-parent households, lack of hope, and crack/cocaine babies, many teachers remain stagnant in their teaching techniques. The kids are dealing with a new set of variables, but some teachers still want the kids to be like they used to be, whatever that means.

On the other end of the spectrum, there are new teachers fresh out of college. Oftentimes these teachers have just finished courses such as Curriculum Methods and the History of Education. These courses ignore the extreme dynamics, unique situations, and poetry in motion that are required to be a highly effective, alternative education teacher. The classroom management courses offered at the university level are often suburban, unrealistic, and ineffective.

This book has a definite niche and purpose. It will enlighten you about alternative education, free choice learning, if you will. What I am presenting are ideas, stories, strategies, and knowledge that I have learned over more than 30 years in and around the classroom.

We can all do a better job. Learning something new is exciting. We all need to be creative, innovative, and caring. We can make things happen.

If a student drops out and does not learn, let's consider it the system's fault. We are a part of that system. Granted, there are dysfunctional homes, terrible conditions, and a political system that works against some excellent educational programs. In the midst of (and in spite of) the chaos, we can change and make a difference. Our focus must be on the powerful, often subtle interaction between teacher and student. This book is about what we can do to help kids. What we do or don't do makes a difference.

1

HISTORY OF ALTERNATIVE EDUCATION

Don't look where you have fallen, look where you slipped.

—African proverb

Education has been a focus of societies throughout history. The idea of a free or public education for all students took effect after much turmoil in America, with various groups fighting a variety of issues to make sure they were part of the American educational system and included in the definition of "all persons."

Alternative education in the United States has a long and complex history. Events across the country and around the world converged to produce the educational choice and parental liberty enjoyed by many Americans and sought by people around the globe.

Let us take a brief journey to explore how and why the movement for wider, more diverse school choice has grown throughout the history of America.

Until the 1830s, America and its Framers relied on an educational tradition of home education, religious schooling, private schooling, and apprenticeship. With the exception of African slaves, who had family members sold in auctions, and the victims of the Massachusetts Bay Colony, who were sometimes deprived of family autonomy, parental rights were strongly protected and families enjoyed complete educational choice.

A change in approach began under President Andrew Jackson. From 1830 onward American Indians suffered under the Jacksonian Paradigm. In the United States, a supposed lack of "civilization" had always been used to justify subjugation of African American families. The same rationale now applied to American Indians, maintaining that they should be "civilized" with federally funded educational programs.

The Mormons, a religious group with many European immigrants, afforded an opportunity to extend the Jacksonian Paradigm from racial minority groups to religious minority groups.

During the same historical period, growing communities of Catholic immigrants and freed African slaves also came into conflict with the dominant white Protestant population. Ethnic, racial, and religious tensions came to a boil all across the country.

It was also at this time that educational reformers in Europe began to debate teacher-centered versus child-centered approaches to learning and schooling. This can be considered background to understanding a major piece of the alternative education process. Maria Montessori presented alternative methods to the traditional European format of strict teachers and harsh discipline by promoting love and understanding and freedom of movement. Educators of the time considered these methods detrimental to discipline.

School reformers of the 1900s in the United States can also be seen as having a major influence on alternative education. Amos Bronson Alcott (1799–1888) founded the Temple School in Boston. He pioneered a child-centered approach that pursued self-knowledge and reflection. He was more concerned with the physical, emotional, and intellectual well-being of the student than with teaching facts. Francis Wayland Parker (1837–1902) was a forerunner to "progressive" education. He used informal methods and promoted a relaxed social atmosphere in school at a time when teachers were strict authoritarian rulers over the classroom, used rigid techniques, and enforced an inflexible discipline and regimentation of students.

At the same time, industrial tycoons, including Henry Ford, Andrew Carnegie, John D. Rockefeller, and J. P. Morgan were the major forces behind the compulsory school attendance movement. The reason for this was to obtain social control over the work force and "civilize" demographic minorities. This led to even more unrest.

Much of what happened in Europe and the American reforms of the 1800s came to influence the so-called progressive education movement in the United States in the 1900s. John Dewey (1859–1952) reiterated what previous innovators believed. His contributions supported such ideas as education should not simply be concerned with intelligence, but also with manual skills and physical/moral development. Dewey felt that education was more than test scores, achievement standards, discipline, and order in the classroom. It was an integral part of life. He also placed an emphasis on experiential/hands-on learning.

Perhaps the most influential event, which was the basic impetus for what is now known as alternative education, was the Eight Year Study. The result of this work came to influence educators to consider "alternatives" to the traditional public schooling style. Conducted during the 1930s and 1940s, students who were attending selected high schools were released from traditional college entrance requirements. The high schools were encouraged to make new curricula and approaches to teaching and learning. Using ideas of Dewey and progressive education, traditional course requirements were replaced with competencies or projects. Special attention was given to their standardized test scores and college entrance exams. The students were also observed during the 4 years after graduation. The results showed that the experimental group scored higher on college entrance exams than the control group. They also tended to be more successful later. These students possessed a higher degree of intellectual curiosity and drive. They were more precise, systematic, and objective in their thinking, participated more frequently in organized student groups, and demonstrated a more active concern with national and world affairs. In the 1970s, this study influenced the climate and curriculum at various schools. In particular, the St. Paul Open School replaced traditional graduation requirements with outcome-based performance competencies (Barr & Parrett, 1995).

As you can see, alternatives in public education have existed since the very birth of American education. Differences based on race, gender, and sexual class set the stage for the constantly evolving nature of the educational system in America.

Alternative schools, recurring organizational experiments that have enjoyed a rich history spanning more than a century, are here to stay.

Urban academies such as Bronx Science, Boston Latin, and San Francisco's Lowell High School have long served families citywide, admitting new students through a competitive admissions process. Yet the Progressive Era in the early 20th century sparked an entirely new kind of alternative school aimed more at revolutionizing the mechanical form of school organization and pedagogy. Curriculum now focused on integrating subject areas, involving students in community service projects, and encouraging children's development in art, drama, and music. The Carnegie Unit for awarding high school course credit was thrown out. Ralph Tyler (evaluation pioneer) and his team also claimed that alternative school graduates outperformed the control group in college and were more active in the social, political, and artistic spheres of collegiate life.

Much of what is regarded as new or innovative in education has a long historical record. Progressive educators tried most of the current practices designed to improve instruction in some form. For example, individual instruction, team teaching, open classrooms, schools without walls, work-study programs, nongraded classrooms, competency-based programs, and alternative schools for secondary students all had their place in educational programs during the 1930s.

Progressives ruled education in the 1930s. They believed that each child was unique and that there were many styles of learning. In some ways, progressive schools were similar to most modern-day alternative schools.

An example of a progressive high school program of the era was the Dalton Plan. This program incorporated Dewey's educational principles, changing schools into an embryonic community that included work study as well as art, history, and science where the child learned intellectual responsibility by selecting and implementing a plan of work and receiving guidance when errors were made. The changes suggested by Dewey led to the development of the progressive curriculum and consequently the Dalton Plan. Also included in the Dalton Plan were methods suggested by Maria Montessori, who believed that children mature at different rates and this should be the foundation of the educational system. The Dalton Plan incorporated these two schools of thought, sought to develop the whole child, and was concerned with physical and social, as well as intellectual, education. This plan included much of the rationale that modern educators use for establishing secondary alternative schools.

Once again, new needs began to emerge after World War II. Critics began to condemn progressive education, the child-centered programs, and permissive practices. A new conservatism in education sprang up. With the rise of industrialism in the United States, schools were modeled after business organizations. Schools became like factories, processing students in the same way that an automobile is processed. Anonymity and detachment became pervasive for students, staff, and community.

In 1947 a group of educators launched the life adjustment movement. This movement became interested in how to meet the needs of those students who seemed not to benefit from standard courses.

New needs again emerged in the 1950s. George Dennison established the first "street school," which was an alternative educational program for minority students from low-income families on New York City's Lower East Side. Half of his students came from the public schools, where they had labels such as severe learning, drop-out potential, and behavior problems. These were students who had been cast off by society and their parents.

The 1950s also went back to a concern for strengthening conservatism and authoritarianism. Progressive education was under fire. Teachers were exhausted by the demands of alternative education. Schools in the early 1950s strove to develop a sense of belonging. They began to individualize.

By the end of the 1950s progressive education ideas faltered. Influenced by events such as the Cold War and especially the Russian launch of the *Sputnik* satellite in 1957, national interests, illustrated by the passage of the National Defense Act of 1958, replaced any vestiges of individual-centered ideas with a subject-centered curriculum. Competing with the Russians meant increased competition in schools, ability grouping, and tracking students according to tests given by school counselors.

It appeared that alternative education had hit a cultural and political nadir. Nonetheless, home education and alternative education did persist in the face of this onslaught, especially among Catholics, Mormons, Mennonites, American Indians, expatriates, and (especially during the 1940s and 1950s onward) an assortment of theologically conservative Protestants.

Prior to 1960 alternative education existed primarily outside the public school system, either in parochial or community/home-based settings. A distinctly different approach began in the 1960s, when civil rights public school critics expressed their concern about the direction of public education. As desegregation gained momentum, public schools were boycotted. This led to the creation of freedom schools in stores and churches. For many, freedom schools offered a glimpse of alternative education designed to meet their needs. This included caring adults, new curriculum, and community involvement.

The free school movement was also initiated during this time period. These schools emphasized individual achievement, as opposed to a community emphasis. The premise for the free school movement was that many children were being alienated in the public school system and should be given the opportunity to explore and learn according to their own interests and abilities. There were no specific learning requirements or set discipline imposed on students and evaluation was conducted to determine if the learning environment facilitated personal development as opposed to learning progress objectives. Most of these nonpublic alternative education movements of the 1960s had very brief life spans.

However, these programs forced educators within the public system to recognize the benefits of nontraditional education principles to develop opportunities for school system–based alternative education. Open schools were a product of this reform movement and were characterized by parent, student, and teacher choice; learning autonomy; self-pacing; noncompetitive evaluation; and child-centered principles. The open schools led the way for schools without walls, schools within a school, multicultural schools, continuation schools, learning centers, fundamental schools, and magnet schools.

Educational revolution began in the relatively affluent, rather complacent early 1960s. Despite educational opportunities that differed based on race, gender, and social class that set the stage for the constantly evolving nature of the educational system in America from the earliest days of the country, alternatives, as we know them in the most modern sense, find their roots in the civil rights movement. African Americans in southern states set up some of the first alternative schools. In northern cities, African Americans set up private alternative schools because of their dissatisfaction with the treatment of their children in the public schools.

Next came the Cold War. Not only was it ideological and military, it was a "technical" war as well. There were "knowledge gaps" and our schools were under fire for creating them. Could our schools keep America technologically ahead of the Soviet Union in the endless Cold War? It was not surprising that the principal focus of the educational reform movement was now on math and science.

However, it took the "discovery of poverty" and the civil rights movement in America to reawaken educators from their unthinking complacency about reforming education, specifically, the discovery of the impact of poverty, racism, and alienation on the mental life and growth of the child victims of these blights. Something more was needed to compensate for what many educators thought of as the "deficit" created by "cultural deprivation."

Yes, the 1960s bred a resurging commitment to alternative schools replete from the Progressive Era. The pedagogical philosophy of John Dewey was revived. By the mid-1960s, new educational thinking, largely rooted in Abraham Maslow's humanistic psychology, was presenting a serious challenge to the bureaucratic, group-processing form of mass schooling. Ivan Illich and Paulo Freire were urging that proper schooling must empower children and adults alike to engage the political process and pursue a more just society. Alternative schools, once again, were to be "child-centered," in contrast to the typical "teacher-centered" public schools.

In 1967, Herbert Kohl created a curriculum from his students' experiences and his own imagination. Kohl claimed success in combining creativity and relevant experiences with academic achievement. He worked with various systems in the creation of alternative schools. Historically, some of the most impressive efforts to achieve excellence in education have been initiated at the local or district levels. Some of these schools created in the 1960s and early 1970s were hailed as models of reform, as ways to restore the allegedly cold and indifferent bureaucracies, which schools had become, to the caring environments necessary for helping the students to learn. The nation's interest in school reform abated in the 1970s, but there remains a steady interest in alternative schools.

The 1970s conception that school should touch the lives of individual children gained credibility. By the mid-1970s "free schools" were operated by parent collectives, schools without walls were opened across the country, and theme schools were developed. This, in turn, led to magnet schools and their selective curriculums (math/science magnets, arts/drama academies, dual-language/humanities programs, and vocational/career academies).

News from some of the early alternatives had been extremely positive, often with impressive success with children who had previously detested school. Through the 1970s and 1980s alternative schools were called on to solve a variety of our nation's ills ranging from crime and delinquency to youth unemployment.

In the 1980s, alternative education conceptualization began to narrow in scope and focused more on conservative and remedial purposes. Many previously successful open schools did not survive this change in the political and societal climate. During this time period, alternative education became geared toward teaching academic basics to improve achievement, and de-emphasized the idea of collective decision making in the educational process.

The 1980s brought open-enrollment options. Minnesota was the first state to enact a statewide open-enrollment scheme. The initiatives varied substantially, especially in the value placed on ensuring all families equal access to education. Minnesota subsidized transportation costs for low-income families. In Massachusetts, the overwhelming majority of participating families were white, and they left racially integrated working-class communities for predominately white and wealthier suburban schools. This was a case of Robin Hood in reverse (state school dollars were pulled from already depressed districts and transferred to wealthier districts).

Not to many years later, educational choice resurfaced in a new package: magnet programs. As schools-within-a-school programs and as stand-alone schools, magnet education developed primarily in response to social and racial inequalities in efforts to integrate the school system. While magnet programs did attract non-neighborhood students into a previously segregated school or area, little actual diversity was accomplished as magnet students were largely separated from neighborhood students by programming.

The 1990s brought vouchers for private and parochial schools. Wisconsin was the first state to authorize an experiment with publicly funded vouchers. Currently, family demand for these municipal voucher programs has clearly outnumbered the availability of choice slots. The 1990s also brought forth the charter school movement. These schools continue to demonstrate innovative pedagogies, enlightened learning, and more potent ways of socializing our youth.

During this decade the dialogue about what alternative education was, what alternative schools should look like, and who should attend them was expanded. The traditional schooling style was not only not meeting the needs of our students, but was also turning off a great majority of them.

During the late 1990s, the alternative educational movement grew enormously, both in terms of numerical quantity and demographic diversity. New technology, including the Internet, satellite networks, and compact discs made alternative education even more convenient. Alternative education began to grapple with new challenges (coping with increasing diversity within the alternative education community and gaining equal access to taxpayer-funded resources and instruction).

Regardless, throughout the 1990s there was little change within public schools. Instead the decade found a renewed growth in alternatives that focused on disruptive, suspended students or students that the traditional schools said lacked effort or needed a change in attitude. This was a reaction to an increase in violence, drugs, gangs, and other issues. These get-back-on-track programs were designed to enable the student to become more successful.

American schools in the 2000s continue to have large numbers of students who drop out because they are bored, poorly adjusted, unable to compete, or merely uninterested in the courses. Numerous school systems are attempting to offer alternative high schools and other alternative programs in an effort to meet the needs of students for whom the regular educational program is unsatisfactory. Alternative education, like a struggling student, is not a new concept though its forms continue to change.

In the past 50 years the role of alternative education has been:

- to develop students' basic skills for vocational preparation not offered in the traditional public school
- to offer smaller classes, with more interaction allowing for greater awareness by students of who they are
- to develop individual talent and uniqueness
- to understand and encourage cultural plurality and diversity
- to prepare students for various roles in our society (consumer, voter, critic, parent, spouse, etc.)
- to be responsive to needs within their communities
- to be flexible and more responsive to change
- to offer relevant curriculum which meets the needs and desires of what students want to learn
- to be more humane to students and teachers, with fewer bureaucratic constraints
- to provide a choice, an alternative to the current school in the community
- to take on students who are not successful in traditional schools

In this age of accountability, the school administration may want to envision alternative schools as viable solutions for potential dropouts as well as unsuccessful traditional school students. Alternative schools typically serve students who are at risk for school failure or are disenfranchised from the traditional school system.

Whether cruising on bikes along suburban sidewalks or atop skateboards on city streets, children humanize our neighborhoods. In turn, the social world of adults springs to life around our children. Alternative education and alternative programs offer an inspiring story about activist parents and teachers eager to create more fulfilling communities for themselves and for their children.

2

SCHOOL CHOICE: TRUST FOR PARENTS' PICKS

> The purpose of life is to live it, to taste experience to the utmost, to reach out eagerly and without fear for newer and richer experiences.
>
> —Eleanor Roosevelt

Touted as an unsinkable ship of social progress for more than a century, public schooling is now listing badly. Achievement is stagnant or declining, public opinion is low, and community conflict over what is taught seems to be ever increasing. Some schools, especially in the inner cities, have already slid beneath the waves, extinguishing the educational hopes and dreams of countless children. Literally thousands of would-be reformers have suggested patches here and there, but the water just keeps flooding in.

If the education of the next generation is not to be completely forsaken, we need to cast aside our assumptions about how schools should be run, and consider not only major overhauls to the current system but also entirely different approaches.

Realistically, we first have to understand people's educational needs before we can determine which sorts of school systems most effectively serve those needs. Public opinion around the world shows that there is a fundamental kernel of agreement among parents on the importance of basic academic subjects. People expect that, as a minimum, their children will have mastered reading, writing, and elementary math by the time they are in high school. There is an equally strong emphasis on career preparation, since parents from Milwaukee to Munich consider landing a good job to be one of the main purposes of education.

Beyond these basics, priorities diverge wildly. Whenever a state-run school system adopts one set of priorities at the expense of all others, conflict inevitably ensues. Consider the battles over religion in the classroom that have plagued the United States for over 100 years, and the rest of the world for centuries before that.

Clearly we need a system that can cater to differences between families, but what about people without school-aged children? To the extent that the general public subsidizes education, by whatever means, it can rightly ask that its needs be met as well. Fortunately, parents and nonparents agree that basic academics and career preparation are the keys. Most people also consider any contribution that schooling can make to the harmony of social relations and the productivity of the economy desirable. Finally, citizens expect to get their money's worth from the schools. If costs increase and taxes are raised, student achievement should go up as well.

Educational reformers have suggested a whole range of strategies for improving our schools, from new curricula and tougher standards, to charter schools, vouchers, and even complete privatization.

We need to know what has worked and what has not, and why. What history shows us is that the problems of high spending, lack of successful innovation, unresponsiveness to the needs of families, and social strife over what is taught are mainly caused by the way public schools are run, not by the people who staff them or the particular standards or curricula they adopt.

It appears to be the absence of competition between schools that stifles innovation and inflates prices, the lack of potential profits that makes applied educational research and development a waste of money and time, and the lack of parental freedom of choice that sets family against family in a bitter fight for ideological control of the schools. Overall, we can have the educational outcomes we want (higher academic achievement, effective innovation, social harmony, responsive teachers, reasonable costs, etc.) if we allow school choice. It is hoped that school choices will help all citizens to assess the merits of the educational system and offer parents the best choice for the future of their children and communities.

Choice abounds in America. It is the cornerstone of our nation. Education is no different. Today's parents face an abundance of choices when deciding where and how to educate their children. This array of options can be both a blessing and a curse.

Choice is growing in popularity. Parents consider options for their children that range from publicly funded private schools to homeschooling, from profit-making schools to charter and magnet schools. All possibilities have their strengths. All deserve consideration if America is serious about renewing its troubled educational system.

In most American cities, a student enrolled in the public school system is assigned to a local school by the district. Parents do not usually select the public school that their child will attend. In recent years, however, a growing number of citizens have backed reformers efforts to allow parents to choose their children's schools. Such "parental choice" alternatives include open-enrollment options, which allow parents to send their child to any public school in their state; charter schools, which are publicly funded schools operated by parents and teachers; and voucher programs, in which parents are given state-funded tuition grants to send their children to private schools.

Choosing the best option for your child is complicated and can be intimidating. Unfortunately, just dropping children off at the neighborhood school without a second thought isn't always the best choice anymore. Since choices do exist, it's important that we become educated about them. The following chapters will cover several school-choice options.

School choice is the slogan of a U.S. movement to give parents more say in which primary and secondary schools their children attend. The movement hopes that increased choice will cause more fierce competition between different schools, and thereby raise the overall quality of education.

School-choice proponents differ in the extent to which they advocate privatization. Some don't advocate it at all, wishing only to allow parents greater choice between different public schools within a district. Others seek to blur the distinction between public and private schools by granting parents the option either of spending vouchers at private (or possibly religious) schools or getting tax credits for doing the same.

The proponents of school choice say that if parents are given a choice about where public money should go, they will pick the better schools and the underperforming schools will have to improve or lose public funding. Proponents claim that school choice is a good way to improve public education at low cost, by forcing schools to perform more efficiently.

Critics argue that tax breaks and vouchers would take away money from the schools that most need financial assistance and that taking money away from them would make the situation at those schools even worse.

Proponents of school choice believe that empowering families with educational options will promote change in how school systems are governed. Choice has been widely adopted, hardly a state in the United States does not have some type of choice plan, and hardly a major urban area does not have a limited choice plan.

In 1988, Minnesota became the first state to enact statewide open enrollment for all students, making all public schools throughout the state open to any K–12 grade student, provided that the receiving school had room and the transfer did not upset racial integration efforts.

Students also have numerous other options. High school juniors and seniors can take courses at public or private institutions of higher education for both high school credit and for college credit. Drop-outs and students at risk of not graduating are offered supportive programs. In addition, families are allowed to claim a tax deduction for school expenses, including private school tuition. The Charter Schools Act permits teachers and parents the right to create and operate new public schools, which are accountable to public authority and parents.

New York City has citywide choice. It has the largest public school system in the nation, consisting of 32 community school districts serving nearly 1.5 million highly diverse students. Parents have the right to transfer their children to any New York City public school, provided space is available. A well-known choice district is District 4, which lies in East Harlem, one of New York City's poorest neighborhoods. Teachers were given the autonomy to redesign and even create new schools. Orientation sessions are offered to parents who are interested in enrolling their children at these schools.

Many districts throughout the nation offer the choice of magnet schools. Students have the choice of academic or vocational magnets or those that combine academic and career programs. These schools have programs that focus on science and engineering, medicine, the performing arts, humanities, law, business, fashion, and other themes. Parent and staff involvement is high, and the students appear to be highly motivated.

Choice in Massachusetts has been seen as a means to achieve racial and ethnic balance in the schools. Experiments with choice grew out of efforts to attract white students to inner-city schools. The family selects a school after receiving information and assignment is made based on family preferences. All students have equal assess to all public schools regardless of geographical location.

Cambridge has one of the most successful choice programs in Massachusetts. The crux of the program is the Parent Information Center, which offers information in six different languages. Students in Cambridge outperform students nationally in reading, math, social studies, and science (Carnegie Foundation, 2004).

Milwaukee, Wisconsin, implemented the nation's first pilot voucher choice plan in September 1990. Selected students are entitled to receive public money to attend any nonsectarian private school of their choice. The cash value of the voucher is equivalent to the state-per-pupil expenditure on public schooling. Parent involvement in school activities is greater in choice schools than in most other Milwaukee public schools (Witte, 2004).

Choice, as shown in the above districts, has proven to be a useful tactic in promoting urban public education transformation and experimentation, and its focus on the involvement of families in all phases of schooling is important.

Inner-city parents and church pastors have joined together with residents of rural areas and homeschoolers in demanding greater educational freedom. Educational vouchers, tuition tax credits, charter schools, and other forms of school choice have garnered the support of a diverse coalition of parents in search of a common end: educational excellence. Public education bureaucrats and many teachers unions remain vigorously opposed to greater educational freedom and the competition and accountability it brings. They would see their monopoly power vastly diminished by reform, in favor of parents and children.

The ideal form of education is one that is freely chosen by parents in accordance with their values and that best meets their child's intellectual, physical, and spiritual needs. Religious and private nonsectarian schools can play an important role here, as a free market in education allowing a wide variety of school concepts takes hold. The most efficient system of education would be one that resembles the free market, as is the case for other goods and services, with many providers to meet the diverse needs.

Through school choice, parents learn to become more actively involved in the decisions surrounding their children's education. They are no longer forced to remain passive figures in the lives of their children while government bureaucrats call the shots. Instead parents are called upon to "shop around" for the best available education in order to meet their child's needs. Parents exemplify responsibility in taking such an active part in their own child's education. This is something that would have been next to impossible for many parents, especially for low-income parents whose children are most in need of a sound education in order to realize their full potential later in life, without a school-choice regime.

More questions arise: Do educational vouchers permit government officials the right to regulate the religious activity in schools, or simply enable parents to purchase an education at the school of their choice? Do tuition credits allow social engineers to encourage one form of educational experience over another or simply enable parents to better afford the education deemed by them most appropriate for their child? Are the freedoms of charter schools dramatically imposed upon by bureaucratic restrictions, or are these publicly funded schools superior to the present system of public schooling?

These are valid concerns that must be examined as the evidence on school choice continues to pour in. A school-choice regime that only entrenches government in education, instead of freeing parents from bureaucratic control, is self-defeating and sows the seeds of its own demise.

Advocating school choice is a way to achieve greater liberty and parental responsibility in education. School choice, in all its many forms, is a prudent step in the right direction, toward restoring the fundamental role of parents in providing an education for their children.

More and more over the last few years, public school systems have been providing parents with a range of choices for their child's education. As previously stated, these choices include transferring to another school within the district; becoming part of a school with a special focus like math and science, often called a magnet school; participating in a charter school or alternative school; attending a private school; homeschooling; and in some cases providing vouchers, providing the parents money to allow their children to enroll in a private school of their choice.

What should one consider when choosing a school option?

There is a lot to think about when choosing the right school for your child. Moving your child to a new school is a big decision. How do you know which option is best for you? Consider:

- Class size. The number of children in each classroom may make a difference in how much your child is able to learn.
- School size. Some children do better in large schools where they have many other children to play with and many choices for classes. Others like smaller schools, where there may be fewer choices for classes, but closer relationships with students and teachers can be made.
- Subject matter. Some schools are able to concentrate more easily than others on specific subject areas, such as sciences or arts.
- Location. The location of a school is important to some parents and students for reasons of safety, convenience, and facilities.
- Test scores. The highest test scores are not always a guarantee that a school and its teachers are good, but they do indicate that children at the school learn more over time than children at schools with the lower test scores.
- Diversity. To some parents it is important for a school to be racially, ethnically, and culturally diverse.

How do I research my school options? In addition to the factors listed above, you need to understand each option before making a decision. One such option is transferring to another public school, perhaps in a different neighborhood. You may find that another public school in a different neighborhood is a better place for your child to learn. Schools are different in different areas so it is important to look at other schools and find one that matches your child's needs. For example, if your child works better in small groups look for a school that may have smaller classroom sizes even though it is a few extra miles away.

Another option is public charter schools. These schools are public schools that are granted a charter or contract to operate as if they are independent for a period of time (usually 3 to 5 years). During the contract period, charter schools are given freedom from regulations that other schools may have to follow. In return for this freedom, charter schools have to produce positive academic results or their sponsor may choose not renew their charter.

Magnet schools are an option. Magnet schools are specialized schools within the public school system that attracts certain types of students. Many magnet schools have good reputations for teaching students, especially in their specialty areas. Students in magnet schools are surrounded by students who have similar interests to their own. Some magnet programs are whole school magnets where all students in the school participate in the program. Others are programs within a larger school setting.

The voucher program is a fairly new option. A voucher is a letter that represents money. The voucher is given to parents to allow them to send their children to a school of their choice. Publicly funded voucher programs use money that would normally go to the regular public schools in order to pay for the costs incurred in going to a private school, a religious school, or for homeschooling.

Homeschooling is another option, where parents educate their children at home rather than sending them to public or private schools. Parents homeschool for a variety of reasons. Most are unhappy with their child's school and feel that they can do a better job educating their child than the school. Some parents do not like the school environment and are concerned about violence or other social issues, and they want to protect their children from those situations. Some parents choose homeschooling to foster a closer family unit. Some children do not learn well in a classroom setting and learn better at home. Homeschooling is a lifestyle and a commitment. Once you decide to homeschool your child, you have to prepare the assignments, plan the classes, teach them, and assess them. It takes a great deal of time and commitment on your part.

You may choose a private school such as a parochial or nondenominational Christian school because you are concerned about your child's religious education. You may want a certain standard of advanced education that your local public school just can't offer, or your own experience in a private school was such that you hope to duplicate that positive experience for your child.

Next you must prepare your child for a new school.

Changing schools is a big deal. It means making new friends, meeting new teachers, and going to a different building and area. Help your child to know what to expect. For example, check out the bus route or subway route prior to their first day. It is important that children feel safe and know where they are going. Talk to your child about being in a new place and meeting new people. It is tough to start anew. Help your child find out what is expected of him or her, how grading works, and if the workload is different. Encourage him or her to stay active by playing a school sport, joining band or choir, and continuing favorite activities. Finally, find out if other children in the same class live close by and try to meet them so your child sees a familiar face that first day at school.

We all have goals for our children. We all have our own philosophy of education. Our actions are a result of what we believe. What kind of person do you hope and pray that your child will grow up to become? His or her schooling choice should nurture that goal and not hinder it.

If your child is currently enrolled in school, you can ask yourself some critical questions to determine whether or not the school furthers the goals you have for your child. Be grateful choices exist. It may have seemed easier when there were no choices with regards to schools, but it wasn't always better. Some of our children have greater needs than their neighborhood school can meet.

Choices create competition, which raises the level of excellence. Choice is a good thing. One of the beauties of choice is that nothing is written in stone. You can always choose again if circumstances or the needs change.

What does my child really need?

Your child's needs are the pivotal pieces in your decision making. Family needs are also a big piece of the pie. What is your child's preferred learning style? What are his or her gifts and talents? Matching your child's education to your child's needs and learning style creates harmony. It decreases frustration and lowers stress levels for all concerned.

If your child is a strong visual learner who is also spatial and needs to move around as he learns, a traditional classroom with a lecture format for teaching will make him or her squirm. He or she will only absorb snippets of information. The better you know your child the better able you are to make the best choice possible for him or her. We tend to put more effort into buying a house in just the right neighborhood with the right amenities (based on family needs) than we do in choosing our child's schooling.

Where children go to school can be an emotional decision. A step-by-step process can take the anxiety out of the decision making. First, define the problem. It can be difficult to put our finger on what exactly is wrong, especially when we are upset. Try to see the real problem in the mess. Next, brainstorm possible solutions or alternatives. Judge them according to whether or not they can solve your problem. Let your creative juices flow, don't censor your ideas, let them come. Develop a plan of action and be prepared to adjust the plans when necessary. Always ask yourself if the mission of the school matches the specific needs of your child, if parent involvement is highly valued, and whether or not the values of the school are in line with your family values.

When looking at private schools, ask yourself if the curriculum is appropriate and challenging enough for your child, are the teachers certified in their subject area, does the learning environment nurture creativity or stifle it, and how much homework is required weekly.

If you are planning to homeschool, ask yourself if your child is ready for school at age 5, socially as well as emotionally. Am I willing to sacrifice my time, give up that "alone" time to always have the children around? Do I have beliefs or values to impart, and am I willing to learn? No matter your background, it takes commitment, love, and the willingness to learn what works and what doesn't work for your child.

Another question you must answer for yourself regarding school choice is: What is my philosophy of education? Schools are created and managed with an emphasis on a particular educational philosophy. Sure, there is always talk about what should or shouldn't be taught in schools.

Everyone is concerned about the values imparted. But as you consider where to place your child for 7 (or more) hours per day, you must also consider the philosophy from which the school is operating.

What is the purpose of education? Answer the question for yourself and then use the answer to help you choose the right school for your child. Your philosophies should match as closely as possible. The following are some directions that schools take in their own philosophies. Find out which one you are considering following. It is one more piece to the puzzle.

- Outcomes-based education (OBE). The intent here is to judge schools not by what goes into them, but what comes out of them, namely, how much and how well children learn.
- Education standards. Standards-based education argues that students are apt to be better educated if those in charge are clear about what exactly the students are supposed to learn.
- Skills versus knowledge. This thinking scorns the idea that students must master certain facts. The argument is that since knowledge is changing so fast nowadays, there is no reason to memorize any of it.
- Multiculturalism. This stresses the importance of children developing knowledge of a number of different cultures and a respect for other people's heritages.
- Developmentalism. This view says that children develop in natural stages at their own pace, and that learning should never be forced on a child. You may hear the term "developmentally appropriate practice" in preschool and primary classrooms. It means that if a lesson is taught too soon it will be a waste of time or even detrimental to the student.
- Cooperative learning. This idea encourages teachers to divide a class into small groups of students who work on assignments together. The group demonstrates what it has learned, and everyone shares in a single grade.

Parents are empowered through school choice. There is no longer any debate over whether parents want choice (they do) and whether they are more satisfied with their child's education once empowered to exercise choice (they are). Mounting research shows that parents both want and know how to make informed choices for their children's education.

Studies from school-choice experiments, including the Milwaukee Parental Choice Program, the Dayton PACE Program, the New York School Choice Scholarship Program, the San Antonio CEO Horizon Scholarship Program, and the Washington Scholarship Fund, show that choice can be an engine for parental involvement.

These studies indicate that parents with children in choice programs attend more school activities, volunteer more in their children's schools, communicate more with teachers, and help more with homework.

On virtually every measure tested, such as school safety, discipline, instructional quality, teacher skills, respect for teachers, class size, and school facilities, parents are overwhelmingly more satisfied with their chosen school than their assigned school. Parents are also more likely to reenroll their child in the chosen school because of their satisfaction with the program.

Americans want to see choice implemented. A survey by Portrait of America in 2004 found that 52% of adults believe that introducing competition by allowing parents to select schools would do more to improve education in America than spending money. Similarly, 54% favor school vouchers, and 59% say that allowing parents a choice in school selection is more likely to produce accountability than oversight by a school board. For years, polls have shown the vast majority of voters favor school-choice programs. Even parents who say they wouldn't change schools if they could believe parents should have the opportunity to choose.

The public education system, not public schoolteachers or administrators, is the greatest barrier to parental involvement. It interferes with the parents' right and responsibility to seek the education they believe is best for their children, and the monopolistic practice of directing all public funding to public schools has fostered indifference among parents, many of whom feel little reason to pay attention when their choices are made for them.

If all parents had the financial ability to choose their child's school, those schools would survive only if they placed students' interests before all else. Teachers and administrators would have to improve their schools through the healthy competition that would evolve in a choice system. More important, school choice places higher expectations on parents.

Today it is fashionable to hold parents responsible for cultivating their child's educational and social progress, but parents have limited authority outside the home to fulfill that duty. Choice frees parents from the shackles of bureaucratic control and increases their ability to participate in their child's overall development.

School choice often comes under fire from teachers' unions. Dire union warnings broadcast that allowing parents more educational options could spell the end of public schools. However, there is a strong constituency of people who believe greater school choice will actually improve education. And as for teachers, there are many reasons to believe that choice will benefit them too. Let's look at the arguments. Critics of school choice argue that allowing more students to leave the public schools will result in teachers being laid off. But a moment's thought reveals a flaw in this argument. Demand for teachers will not decrease just because more parents choose to send their children to different schools. And these different schools are likely to be in the same general area of the schools that the students are leaving. So if jobs are lost at the old schools as a result of a mass student exodus, the new schools will need to hire more teachers to meet their growing demand.

There is even the possibility that greater school choice would result in more jobs for teachers. How? As competition among schools intensifies, administrators will need to come up with ways to attract more students. One of the selling points many schools employ is that of smaller class size. As more schools offer smaller classes as an incentive to parents, more teachers would be needed to keep the teacher-to-pupil ratio low.

Another claim of school-choice critics is that choice will necessitate many changes that are disruptive to the educational process. True, but that can be a good thing. Teachers are used to adapting to new situations. They have a new batch of students every year, sometimes twice a year. They adapt to innovative teaching methods and ideas all the time. Sometimes this happens formally with training and in-service, but more often it is done informally. A teacher picks up a new idea from a colleague, a magazine article, a parent, or even a student. The "disruptions" caused by school choice will only enrich the cross-fertilization of ideas, to the benefit of the students.

Choice programs can allow teachers to improve and do their jobs better. Most teachers agree that new ideas and new situations are what make their jobs exciting and fun. Too many teachers tell stories of how they've been pressured, if not intimidated, into altering or abandoning something they believed in because of bureaucratic interference.

When school choice forces schools to listen to the teachers, the teachers will be a part of the changes that will inevitably occur.

Finally, critics argue that school choice will mean pay cuts for teachers. This is an unlikely scenario. The private sector pays more and since school-choice money follows the students, parents who can afford several thousand dollars a year in tuition under a voucher or tax-credit plan will find them in the private school market. A lot of that new money will go to teachers, as competing schools scramble to attract and retain the best educators they can find. Teachers do not need to fear school choice. The evidence shows that it will benefit them as well as their students.

Genuine competition is our best hope for a better K–12 education system. In a truly competitive setting, public and private schools would compete equally for customers. Parents would be able to choose equally among public and private schools.

Currently, school-choice programs appear as nothing more than escape valves for low-income children trapped in the worst inner-city schools. We should seek school choice for all children. The dream of creating a higher standard of quality for both private schools and public schools can become a reality, but only if we set a goal of a choice system that will improve government-owned and private schools.

Desperate times require desperate measures. We can learn a lesson from Martin Luther King Jr. as the school-choice battle gets intense. It will take action, not armchair radicalism to convince policy makers that parents really want more educational choices. King outlined the steps for nonviolent social change. School-choice advocates should look to these steps for guidance. Step one is information gathering. King wrote that those who want to make social change should look at the facts to see if social injustice exists. In 1963 America there clearly was injustice against blacks. It is clear today that many public schools fail to provide a quality education for many (not a few of whom are black Americans). We have all seen the data showing 55% of blacks and 53% of Hispanics graduate from high school compared to 81% of whites (Education Week, 2006).

Step two is negotiation. Start discussions about the status quo. In school districts around the country, parents have complained about schools that have failed to educate their children. Some of them, who do not want to negotiate with the system, have fled to private schools, or decided to try homeschooling. Step three is self-purification. This step asks participants to consider what their level of personal commitment will be. What are parents willing to do to demonstrate their demand for school choice?

Finally, step four is direct action. The civil rights movement used several types of direct action: sit-ins, demonstrations, and boycotts. King said that he agreed with his critics that negotiation is better than direct action, but, ironically, it is direct action that leads to negotiation. The beauty of school choice is that it is a form of direct action. Once parents have school choice, they will no longer have to negotiate or renegotiate with a recalcitrant status quo.

Like Martin Luther King Jr. and his civil rights struggles, school-choice advocates need to heed the words of Frederick Douglass who said, "If there is no struggle, there is no progress."

Locally and nationally there is an increasing, many-sided concern over the state of American education. From crisis in the inner cities to general academic underachievement, to ethical relativism, to remoteness from parental control, to burgeoning bureaucracies and bloated budgets with corresponding tax burdens, educational problems confront us. And there is a growing perception that these problems reflect the monopoly-financing environment out of which they have come. That monopoly artificially protects the public schools from normal competition and comparison, thus encouraging bad habits, and it endangers independent schools cut off from the normal funding. Thus, public schools suffer in terms of educational quality, and independent schools suffer, often unto death, from underfunding.

And, just as the vices of monopoly funding are becoming clearer, so is the ability of choice to break the monopoly and help rid us of its vices. By permitting parents to allocate tax dollars, choice would end the monopoly of assignment. In the same motion, it would reestablish parental control, and it would introduce comparison and competition, the normal human stimuli which encourage excellent performance and cost restraint.

Add to these facts the truth that choice has no downside risk, since any positive educational idea can be explored under it. After all, it is simply "nature taking its course" in education. Parents free to choose without financial penalty will choose schools, public or private, which they judge best for their children, and a natural variety of educational options and models will arise reflecting America's pluralism.

When the contemporary school-choice movement started several years ago, its leading protagonists probably could have met comfortably in a telephone booth. In an amazingly short period of time, it has grown into one of the most sophisticated, passionate, and ecumenical movements in American history. I've never encountered a group of people, activists, philanthropists, public officials, clergy, lawyers, teachers, and parents who are so motivated by good faith, willing to put aside ideological differences in pursuit of a common cause. That is probably why the movement has come so far so fast.

The school-choice movement has widespread, diversified political appeal. It enables low-income and minority families to avoid poorly run and overcrowded schools; infuses free market, competitive principles into a sluggish public educational system; allows individual families, not bureaucratic school systems, to have more control over which schools their children attend and what services are provided there; is considered a low-cost solution to what are considered enormous problems in public education; is purported to lead to better matches between pupil needs and school offerings; and it may increase parent involvement in education.

The school-choice struggle has been fought on many fronts. The decisive battles have come in the courtroom, yet whatever the legal issues in a particular lawsuit, the core argument throughout has been that parents, not government, should have the primary responsibility and power to determine where and how their children should be educated.

The stakes are enormous. For the education establishment, the cause is about jobs and power. For the parents, and for society, the stakes are much higher. Over half a century after *Brown v. Board of Education*, nearly half of all black and Hispanic children in inner-city schools have a much greater likelihood of winding up on welfare or in jail than going on to college or to a productive lifestyle. That is because our K–12 system of education, especially in large urban centers, is a government monopoly much more responsive to special-interest demands than in satisfying consumers. Until we alter the distribution of power, we will consign additional generations of children to educational cesspools. In climbing out from this morass, we should not worry about whether a particular reform proposal is too radical; we should worry about whether it is radical enough.

At its essence, the school-choice movement is a civil rights crusade, an effort to vindicate the sacred and unfulfilled promise of equal educational opportunities. It is not just about ideas, but also about the real lives of real people. Over the years I've met hundreds of low-income parents in cities across America. Many are single parents; few have high school diplomas, let alone college degrees. But they know that in order for their children to succeed, they must somehow secure for them a high-quality education. Unfortunately, the system has written them off, both parents and their children. Too often, the public schools are hostile to low-income parents and assume that they are part of the problem, not part of the solution. The schools assume the children are incapable of learning and subject them to low expectations.

In alternative schools and private schools, both parents and children are transformed. The parents are not discouraged from involvement; they are required to play a role in the school and in their children's education. The students are expected to behave and expected to achieve, and they do. I've walked the hallways of dozens of inner-city alternative schools and visited private schools. The biggest difference is in the children's faces. Regardless of the obstacles they face in their lives outside of school, they are kids who are going somewhere. That look of self-confidence, of determination, of earned pride is all the fuel, all the reward that I could possibly desire.

School choice will not single-handedly solve all education-related problems, namely uneven resources and broken and dysfunctional families, both of which make the dream of a level playing field for all children difficult to achieve. But educational choice is an obvious and inevitable cure for much of what ails us.

In our media-intensive culture it is not difficult to find differing opinions. Thousands of newspapers and magazines and dozens of radio and television talk shows offer differing points of view. The difficulty lies in deciding which opinion to agree with and which "experts" seem the most credible.

Thomas Jefferson once stated that the "difference of opinion leads to inquiry, and inquiry to truth." You must examine the facets of school choice (charter schools, magnet schools, private schools, homeschooling, vouchers, etc.) and examine them with skill and discernment. The choice is yours.

3

ALTERNATIVE SCHOOLS: A SCHOOL OF ONE'S OWN

> We don't have a child to waste. We will not be a strong country unless we invest in every one of our children. All children are essential to America's future.
>
> —Marian Wright Edelman

When Cesar was in the ninth grade, his career ambition was to become an assassin. His credentials were impressive, urban gang member, hardened street fighter, handgun aficionado. Dozens of his friends and family were in prison, dead, or on their way. Even his mother was resigned to his downfall. Three years later he was a captivating poet with a scholarship to a private college.

Cesar graduated from a unique public alternative school in Orange County, California, that has no classes, no grades, no tests, and no easy rides. With guidance from adults, each student builds a customized education program focused on five learning goals (communication, social reasoning, empirical reasoning, quantitative reasoning, and personal qualities). The school's goal is to create versatile, motivated learners.

Students at Cesar's school study fewer topics, but those studied are done so in far more depth. They work closely with adults inside and outside of school. Instead of taking tests, they give public exhibitions of what they've learned. Instead of letter grades, students receive detailed narratives written by their teachers.

Mandy has bleak memories of her days spent at Martinsville High School. She is dyslexic and writes slowly, needing more time than the average student to complete assignments. Mandy would stay up until 3 a.m. doing homework, and she would still not get half of it done. Discouraged, she dropped out of school at age 16. Two years later Mandy found a new academic home at Hammons Off-Campus High School in Martinsville, Indiana. Off-Campus is an alternative school that has helped turn her life around. "I'm going to get my diploma and then study to become a veterinarian. Without Hammons help I would never have gone back to school."

Alternative schools like Hammons are helping kids like Mandy realize their potential. For students who come from homes where academics aren't stressed, who are teen parents, or who need extra help and attention, alternative schools are proving to be a better choice than traditional school settings.

Since the 1983 publication of the famous indictment of American public education, *A Nation at Risk*, authored by the National Commission on Excellence in Education, reference has been made of our failing schools in the media and in policy makers' statements. The belief is widespread that students' levels of achievement are much lower than ever, that most teachers are substandard, and so on. In short, the prevailing view is that our public education system has changed for the worse and that it is now a disaster. That is the problem, pure and simple.

Defining the problem as a "failure" suggests that someone is to blame. It is widely assumed that if schools are failing, then educators must be at fault. I see profound demoralization among teachers. They feel castigated and victimized by the public. Feeling blamed without cause, some strike back. The conversation goes like this . . . high school teachers blame middle school teachers saying, "How can I teach kids to write an essay if you haven't even taught them to write a good paragraph?" Middle school teachers turn around and tell elementary teachers, "How can I teach these kids to write a decent paragraph if you haven't even taught them to write in complete sentences?"

Then all teachers seem to agree that it's the parents fault. After all, parents aren't doing an adequate job of raising their children. Educators say, "If only parents would give me kids who are ready for school and motivated to learn, then I could teach them."

The shame-and-blame game goes on in schools and communities everywhere. The result is that the people who most need to be working together for the benefit of children, educators, and parents, are often feeling more and more isolated, disheartened, and at odds with one another.

Some of us who went to public schools 30 or 40 years ago and remember being challenged and having classmates who wanted to learn forget a critical fact, our public schools are sorting machines, by design. Kids have always been "tracked" according to preconceived ability, as measured by standardized tests, in most schools in this country. We rarely saw the kids in other tracks or those who dropped out.

What is apparent today is that kids who drop out or who are in other tracks or other schools are no longer as invisible as they once were. These students are more visible today because they are being left behind in the new economy. The achievement gap will not be fixed by simply instituting a tougher achievement test. Historically, our schools have never provided equal opportunities to the poor and minority populations in this country. Both school facilities and teachers in poor and minority neighborhoods have always been inferior to those that middle-class white children enjoyed. That's part of what the civil rights movement was about and what the 1954 *Brown v. Board of Education* Supreme Court decision attempted to address.

The achievement gap remains. Because of the increased emphasis on passing high-stakes tests, schools do not have time to teach much that is not on the tests. Worst of all, test results tell us little about the qualities of mind and heart that matter most for success and happiness in adult life.

Our challenge is in dealing with the future. A tug-of-war exists between those who believe that the best way to deal with change is to cling to remnants of the past and those who eagerly embrace the future.

We must face the new challenges that change brings to education while strengthening those values that are most important to us.

The question of how to provide the best education for all America's schoolchildren has compelled a vast array of educational research and experimentation throughout the second half of the 20th century. As questions are debated, new policies and practices have been implemented and yet more questions emerge, resulting in new approaches to education. During the past two decades, in particular, reforms have flourished as the nation has called for high levels of accountability within the educational system. Public school choice, teacher preparation tests, and graduation standards are among the many reforms or policies that have been implemented to enable students to reach their academic potential. Even with these changes, some students are not reaching the academic goals desired by parents, educators, and the public.

More and more educators and policy makers are contending that, if an alternative education option is provided for students at risk of school failure, they will be able to succeed. Advocates argue that alternatives to the traditional school model are imperative to meeting the needs of all students (Barr & Parrett, 2001; Natriello, McDill & Pallas, 1990; Raywid, 1989; Wehlage & Rutter, 1987; Young, 1990).

Alternative schools have been implemented in recent years to address the issue. However, alternative programs have been in place for several decades. They have evolved since the 1960s to the present and are currently a popular educational alternative for many students across the nation.

While there is no precise accounting of alternative programs in the United States, educators estimate that there are over 25,000 alternative schools and programs currently in operation, most designed to reach students at risk for school failure. Alternative education is one important answer to meeting the needs of disenfranchised youth.

Alternative schools and programs have evolved over the years to mean different things to different audiences. One definition for alternative education programs is a separate program within a K–12 public school district established to serve and provide youth whose needs are not being met in the traditional school setting a choice or option. The term *alternative schools* broadly refers to public schools which are set up by school districts to serve populations of students who are not succeeding in the traditional public school environment. Alternative schools offer students who are failing academically or who may have learning disabilities or behavioral problems an opportunity to achieve in a different setting. While there are many different kinds of alternative schools, they are often characterized by their flexible schedules, smaller class sizes, smaller teacher-pupil ratios, and modified curricula.

Three indispensable goals are universal for alternative schools: students attend by choice, the schools are responsive to unmet local needs, and the student body reflects the racial and socioeconomic mix of the community.

In other words, an alternative school is a school that differs from traditional schools in curricula, purpose, or teaching methods. Alternative schools are generally described as maintaining small size, emphasizing one-on-one interaction between teachers and students, creating a supportive environment, allowing opportunities for student success relevant to the students' future, and allowing flexibility in structure and emphasis on student decision making.

Most alternative schools establish a less formal relationship between teachers and students. They make greater use of community resources outside the school and involve parents in the educational process. These schools developed due to dissatisfaction with the quality and goals of traditional schools.

Many alternative schools in the United States operate independently of the public school system. Emphasis is often on allowing students to make their own decisions. Other alternative schools operate as part of the public school system. Such schools may be in one area of a public school building or in a separate building provided by the district. These schools are called magnet schools or specialty schools.

Not all alternative schools have the same goals and the same ways of presenting learning opportunities. Many educators who believe in alternative schools want to provide the opportunity for a different kind of education for the children who would benefit from it.

One major feature of many alternative schools is the open-space classroom. The teacher, instead of lecturing, helps students find interesting and relevant ways to learn on their own. The students work independently or in small groups and the teacher is available to give individual help.

Some examples of alternative schools that are in response to various student needs are street academies and dropout centers that function in poorer sections of many large cities and help high school students and dropouts to continue their education. Storefront schools have developed from child-care and kindergarten facilities. Work schools hold academic classes part of the day and then students work at regular jobs the rest of the day.

Schools without walls, located in many urban centers, take advantage of the educational support provided by businesses and community organizations. Students may spend part of the day at an artist's studio, a factory, a museum, a newspaper office, a repair shop, a theater, or a government or private agency. The purpose of this method is to make learning more realistic and enjoyable and to broaden the experiences offered to high school students.

Some alternative schools emphasize the study of the culture and history of a particular culture/ethnic group. Others seek students from different cultures and ethnic groups.

Alternative schools have been set up throughout the history of American public education and were labeled experimental schools prior to 1960. The term *alternative school* first came into widespread use during the 1960s and referred to a wide variety of programs and institutions that differed greatly from private schools and even special programs within public schools. Most private schools of the 1960s had been established for the children of wealthy families. Most special programs worked only with students who had special needs or exceptional ability. The alternative schools welcomed all students.

African American groups in the Southern states set up some of the first alternative schools. During the 1960s these groups established Freedom Schools in communities where public schools refused to admit black children. In many Northern cities, African Americans set up alternative schools because of dissatisfaction with the treatment of their children in the traditional public schools.

Many people began to realize that a public school system could harm rather than help some children. They declared that parents and educators should have the freedom to develop alternative educational methods.

During the late 1960s, several groups created open space classrooms modeled after the United Kingdom's Infant Schools. Children attend such schools from ages 5 to 7. In the United States, similar classrooms were set up in a number of public schools. Their success contributed to the growth of the alternative school movement.

Alternative educators are aware that they can play an important role in making our society fairer for all students. But we must remember that a student's social class background, gauged by his or her mother's educational level, family income, and ethnicity are the strongest predictors of his or her academic success. The average African American or Hispanic second grader in this country reads at a proficiency level that is already one year behind the typical white child. In this scenario, alternative schools are most beneficial as they use innovative methods to assist these children.

More and more students are being labeled at risk in our educational system. These students are often behind academically, have dropped out of school, or have been suspended or expelled from conventional schools. Some states have implemented school-choice options that address the needs of these students, giving them a choice of an alternative school setting. These programs, commonly referred to as "second-chance" programs, are designed to address the specific needs of at-risk students. The second-chance option combines the pedagogy of alternative programs with the philosophical orientation of school choice offering a "second chance" to those who are failing in the traditional system.

Alternative programs and schools are an integral part of the second-chance option. Yet, little is known about the characteristics of these programs and how they relate to school choice. While other types of school-choice options have received the majority of attention over the past few years, second-chance programs have been quietly addressing the needs of students most disenfranchised from the traditional system.

Alternative has meant different things to different people over the past several years. As early as 1978, the controversy over the definition of *alternative* was acknowledged. Nearly 30 years later there is still discussion about what alternative means.

Alternative programs fall into three categories. Type I alternatives are schools of choice and are usually popular. They sometimes resemble magnet schools and in some locales constitute some or all of the choice systems (charter schools, schools without walls, experiential schools, career-oriented schools, dropout recovery programs, after-hours schools, and theme location schools). They are likely to reflect programmatic themes or emphasis pertaining to content or instructional strategy or both. They use innovative programs or strategies to attract students. Type I programs tend to focus on the match between program and students, not simply on correction of a problem with the student. Other characteristics include deregulation, flexibility, autonomy, teacher and student empowerment, multiple teacher roles, small in size, self-paced instruction, and support services.

Type II alternatives are programs to which students are sentenced, usually as one last chance prior to expulsion. These are not schools of choice and their emphasis is typically on behavior modification or remediation. Type III alternatives are for students who are presumed to need academic or social/emotional remediation or rehabilitation or both. The assumption is that after successful treatment students can return to mainstream programs.

Examples of alternative programs from various states across the nation give a glimpse of the variety and scope of the alternative educational options available today.

Michigan alternative schools are designed to meet the needs of students at risk. The state has a clear policy of choice for the programs and a goal of maintaining populations in the alternative schools that reflect the social/ethnic makeup of the communities in which they operate.

Minnesota has alternative programs available that will help students who are at risk of not graduating from their traditional school. Students, kindergarten through adult, may enroll in the programs, many of which are offered year-round. The programs range from public alternative programs and area-learning centers to privately contracted alternatives. Students may qualify for the programs if they are performing substantially below their grade level on achievement tests, speak English as a second language, are pregnant or parenting, are chronically truant, or are one year behind their age group in school. Programs maintain a small size and are staffed by teachers who specialize in educating at-risk students. New York includes students with behavioral or academic difficulties, highly performing students, newly immigrated students, and students who may be pregnant or parenting as part of their alternative programs.

North Carolina's alternative learning programs exist as separate classrooms within an existing high school or in a separate school away from the campus. These schools were developed to meet the needs of students experiencing discipline or behavior problems, attendance issues, and academic difficulties in the regular school setting.

Ohio alternative programs provide a range of short-term and long-term options for students and may include social skills building, health behavior training, career development, general educational development (GED) completion, day suspension, and correctional programming. The programs appear to be exclusively designed for students who are having academic difficulty or have dropped out of school.

South Carolina alternative programs are considered last-chance options and use self-paced, computer-assisted, whole-group, traditional, and tutorial instructional formats. Ninth graders make up the largest percentage of students in these programs.

The State of Washington has alternative options ranging from Internet schools to schools for incarcerated youth. The state has maintained alternative schools as schools of choice rather than schools of remediation or "last-chance" placement. One of the fastest growing alternatives in the state, Parent Partner Programs, combines homeschooling and public education components for students.

Alternative schools seek to change students' attitudes about schooling, reinforce basic literacy skills, reduce incidences of truancy, and remove disruptive or noncompliant students from the regular classrooms. New teaching methods, teaching styles, and curriculum development have served as ways to attract students who will now fight for these educational privileges. With funding in place to establish programs, the states began adopting measures to fit what its officials thought necessary. Currently, states offer an individualized, nontraditional curriculum greatly varying in coursework and scheduling. All states want their alternative programs to redirect students' lives. They want their programs to enable students to continue in the educational process, remain in school, avoid dropping out, return to normal classroom environments if agreeable, obtain a high school diploma or the equivalent, and to become lifelong learners.

PROGRAM BENEFITS AND BARRIERS

The most commonly found benefit of alternative schools is that they develop methods to keep at-risk students involved in school in a student-centered atmosphere. Other benefits include increasing student productivity, increasing overall school safety, decreasing school violence, increasing parental involvement in school, and providing a greater community atmosphere for all students. By increasing the academics offered to the students, employment opportunities also increase whether through specific vocational training and school-to-work options, or by allowing students more ways to obtain diplomas. Additional benefits found associated with the alternative programs were increased basic skills, increased competencies, increased personal and vocational skills, and increased communication, coping, and self-control skills.

The main barrier to any alternative program is inadequate funding. Other barriers include the community, school and professional attitudes about students and staff, a general lack of understanding of the efforts by the public, problems about who should be included and involved in the programs, and a lack of interagency support (e.g., better cooperation and communication with the juvenile justice system or the state educational system).

The lack of consistency guiding alternative education makes comparing programs difficult. To help alleviate this problem, I would recommend:

- Developing and adopting a broad definition of who should attend the program. Will the program target at-risk students? Behaviorally challenged students? Academically challenged students?
- Agreements between schools, parents, community members, students, and social service agencies need to be explicit. The success of the students and the program hinges on the successful collaboration of all the individuals in the lives of the students.
- Training and development should be put in place for teachers and administrators associated with the program.
- Give students new ways to learn.
- Allow the program to be as inclusive as possible.
- Establish specific entrance and exit criteria. Students, parents, teachers, and administrators must be aware of how students will be sent to, enrolled in, recommended for, or volunteer for the alternative program.
- Establish a systematic evaluation plan.

With the diversity in alternative education and the No Child Left Behind legislation, we must determine what the best alternative education system is rather than simply attempting to put in place any measure to address at-risk students.

Alternative schools are about how to learn in different ways. The following are examples of successful alternative schools operating in the United States today.

The Day and Night School, a last-chance alternative school in Greensboro, North Carolina, is one example of success. With a nontraditional schedule, small classes, and student-centered instruction in a caring environment, the staff implements their philosophy and mission of "meeting students' daily needs." The main reason students are referred to the Day and Night School is sporadic attendance at their home school. However, Day and Night's school climate, classroom environment, and mentoring satisfy the students' sense of belonging, friendship, and self-actualization. The Day and Night School reflects the most positive aspects of effective alternative schools in meeting students' social and emotional needs. The students have fewer discipline problems and are exhibiting less violence. Students like the school, they are doing their work, and they are going on to graduate. Students feel that they are receiving a better education than in their traditional schools.

Jackson School, Jackson, Mississippi, serves suspended sixth, seventh, and eighth graders. The school is located on three sites, each housing a single grade. This transition alternative school emphasizes academics, although mainly it wants students to see how their behavior disrupts the classroom and the school, to see how their behavior antagonizes the authority figures, and to realize how power dynamics work in authoritative relationships. The goal is to help students to develop and internalize a series of coping skills that will enable them to better deal with power/authority and thus avoid getting into crisis situations similar to the ones that got them sent to Jackson. The school's philosophy is to provide consistency, attention, and care. Believing that discipline is the most effective way to achieve behavioral change, the staff focuses, almost exclusively, on individual accomplishments rather than on the large-scale curriculum design. The staff describes the work they do as relying heavily on patience and the ability to see the goodness in a child when no one else has been able to.

Exploration Alternative High School, Ashland, Oregon, (patterned after a school in western North Carolina) serves 15 to 20 at-risk students who are in academic and other difficulties in regular high school due to abandonment, neglect, drug abuse, violent acting out, absenteeism, or learning difficulties. Using a philosophy of low tolerance and high expectations, the program staff creates a community spirit to facilitate social skills and help students succeed academically. The school uses informal, group-based learning, a constructivist approach, coupled with individual instruction based on multiple learning styles concepts. The school goes on field trips one or two days a week, uses hands-on learning balanced with work on computers and worksheets. The student's efforts are collected for their portfolios. The small class size allows for shared decision making. Student success is high.

New Directions Academy, El Paso, Texas, is an extremely popular program, operating under a special waiver from the state, allowing students a flexible choice of attending school a minimum of two hours per day. The program serves students ages 17 to 21. The philosophy of New Directions Academy is to put students first and the academics will follow. Treating students like mature young adults, teachers expect the students to take responsibility for their education. By choosing New Directions, by being assertive, and by taking control of their school, students no longer blame the school system for their lack of achievement. A nurturing climate and individualized attention provides the spirit of community necessary for the sense of belonging many need to feel secure enough to reengage in the learning process.

Minnesota's Area Learning Centers are schools of choice that serve youth through flexible innovative programming that allows students to finish high school courses at their own pace. Innovation and acceleration are more compelling themes than remediation. The schools emphasize the power that choice has to play in the success of the students who are most disenfranchised by the traditional system.

New Paths Area Learning Center, Crookston, Minnesota, is an example of an area-learning center offering students in grades 9–12 a chance to complete credits toward their high school diplomas. This is a program for students who have fallen behind in their coursework, have dropped out and want to return to complete their high school education, or have not been successful in a traditional high school setting.

New Paths focuses on individual learning styles using the independent study attendance model to meet students' needs. A low teacher-student ratio, group interaction, computer resources, employability skills, work experience, and counseling assist students in their transition to postsecondary education or the world of work. Students are assisted in reaching their goals in an open, caring environment, where teachers provide personal attention and promote student responsibility for achievement and self-discipline.

We can see quite clearly how alternative schools can offer a completely different kind of school experience that can be oriented to particular groups. Choice, flexible scheduling, learning styles (computer-based learning, individual or small groups, self-paced independent studies, vocational components), caring teachers (who are also there by choice), and small class size, all complemented by a sense of autonomy, self-control, and responsibility by students for their education.

Educators, politicians, school board members, parents, and community members are coming together and are starting to recognize and value the importance of creating nontraditional options to help meet the needs of all students.

As a nation, we have established institutions of learning that cater to the needs of some. Our schools allow a select handful of students to succeed. Certain segments of our population appear to be at greater risk than others. The future does not bode well for young black and Latino men and women who do not make it through high school.

Of course it is not only black and Latino students who are lost in the educational shuffle. There are hoards of students who simply do not fit into the traditional public school paradigm. Whether this poor fit is the result of an unorthodox learning style, an emotional disability, or a need for a higher level of teacher involvement, these students are often failed. Such students may stay in school but they receive a substandard education.

Virginia Woolf, in her essay, "A Room of One's Own," makes a strong case for schools which cater to the needs of students who are failed by our existing system. She believes in the worth of all students. Bill Lamperes, a man passionately devoted to alternative education, also holds the opinion that all children can be taught. Every child possesses his or her own guides and their guides determine how that child should be taught. These children are in desperate need of schools of their own. Their teachers, who simply do not know what to do with them, too often ignore students with nontraditional learning styles.

America's public schools, in theory, exist to educate all. However, our schools do not honor all students and as a result they cannot educate all. Multiple truths (learning styles, intelligences, cultural traditions) are something many Americans, including educators, have met with resistance. Our dualistic society refuses to see various gradations of value, human success cannot be sustained on many fronts. The very nature of winning, according to western tradition, demands that someone must also lose. Students are rarely judged, nor can they self-assess, by their own merits. A student's performance is weighted in relation to his or her peers. The idea that one must fail for another to win prevails.

Education that does not pit student against student results in the liberation of the mind and ideas.

If an at-risk student makes it to an alternative school, their struggles are not over. Many students are members of a minority group or female or come from a low socioeconomic background. These three segments of society have little representation in traditional school curriculum.

Our society does not readily accept change. Those in power are constantly seeking new and better ways to maintain their power. Those who attempt to move from a position of subservience to a position of self-sustenance are met with hostility. A young black man who attempts to better himself is often considered "uppity." A young woman who decides she wants to study engineering is met with remarks about her femininity. Such remarks suggest to students that they are doing something wrong, something ill-suited to them.

Many students who make it to alternative schools are not safe from prevailing attitudes regarding race, gender, intelligence, and "proper" schooling. Many have been tracked in remedial classes. If you track a student into a remedial group for long enough, success in English will elude him or her. Once that student arrives at an alternative school, it takes a great deal of unteaching and relearning before they come to understand that they can succeed. Once their confidence is built, they are met with resistance from the dominant culture.

Many people actually believe alternative schools have retired hippies teaching drugged-out kids in rooms decorated with beanbag chairs.

They believe that students in alternative schools are not held to the same standards as students in traditional schools. Many believe that the students are never tested and never write papers. Ultimately, most people, if you asked them, would not want their children to attend an alternative school. Students who do attend are still met with a series of guffaws that don't stop even when they choose to remain in school.

The concept of alternative education is not a new phenomenon. In one form or another, education alternatives have existed since American education's earliest beginnings, coming into their own within public education during the latter half of the 20th century. Today, alternative education is thriving as more and more communities see the merit of educating all youth to be responsible members of society.

Alternative education comes in many flavors and is known by as many names and titles as there are programs. Today, best practices in alternative education focuses primarily on utilizing positive, proactive measures to improve student success. Many programs demonstrate that these students thrive in a learner-centered, creative environment that provides a multifaceted program connecting the student to success both academically and socially.

We cannot ignore alternative schools. The public is no longer satisfied with the status quo. This is illustrated by the persistent discussion and debate over privatization, charters, tuition tax credits, vouchers, options, and alternatives.

Consequently, the questions are no longer if and when various options to the traditional public schools will emerge, but what kind. This is a good place to be. Those involved with alternative education have an opportunity to prove the value of their approach to education.

Alternative schools have evolved from a promise made within the American educational system, the promise to educate all students, no matter their circumstances or educational issues. Since the beginning, alternatives have been difficult to describe in philosophy and practice, and the challenge only grows as alternatives expand across the nation. Those who have watched and supported the movement realize its potential to provide a caring, nurturing, hopeful environment for the success of the many involved students.

Dramatic stories are told of students who were on the verge of completely dropping out of school and then found the setting and relationships they needed at alternative schools. Alternative schools allowed them to experience success.

A successful future for alternative schools depends on how we define what success means. To make this definition we must reflect on past history, conduct thorough needs assessment in the present, and lay the groundwork for empirical research and systematic evaluation of alternative schools for the future. Alternative education can be strengthened by its successes, directed toward positive change, and guided by innovation and creativity.

Before alternative schools, our definition of education was narrow. Educators believed that everyone learned in the same way and should be taught in the same way using a common curriculum. We thought that children and their parents were incapable of making decisions about what and how the children learned. We now realize that we were wrong, that there is no single best way for all to learn. We also realize that though alternative education works for some, it is not necessarily best for everyone. Not everyone should be in the same traditional classroom, but the inverse is also true. Alternative schools helped us understand that different students could learn better in very different ways.

This will be the legacy of alternative education, that it was the rainbow lens through which citizens viewed their schools to see if America was living up to its promises, especially equal educational opportunity. Alternative education has set a benchmark that will be used to judge, challenge, and resolve any interest, biases, or agendas that would keep our children from developing their talents, using their abilities, and reaching their full potential.

Traditional education has brought the United States this far. Yet, characteristically, it was limited and exclusive because its definition of education was too narrow. Now American education must embrace diversity. It must respect and nurture variety. It must bring its promised equity to education. And it will. Alternative education is the American education.

4

CHARTER SCHOOLS: A BEACON OF HOPE

> Your children are the sons and daughters of life's longing for itself. You may give them your love, but not your thoughts. For they have thoughts of their own.
>
> —Kahlil Gibran

Margarita Ortiz was a hero long before she started a charter school. Whenever she entered a classroom or assembly, Ortiz signaled a warm sense of caring, quickly engaging the issue at hand. She was consumed by a commitment to her teachers and students, children who flocked to her school from the rising number of Latino households packed on top of each other in apartments and tiny postwar houses not more than a mile from downtown Oakland, California. Ortiz, a longtime elementary school principal, was trusted by these immigrant parents, who struggled to raise their children right, a difficult task on this concrete-gray patchwork of city blocks chopped into disparate pieces by freeway on-ramps and overpasses, surrounded by neglected and drooping chain-link fences.

Affection for Ortiz went even deeper as she boldly led the emancipation struggle, arm in arm with the parish priest, the city's corporate leaders, and outspoken parents, to create one of California's first charter schools in 1993. This slight woman, with fading auburn hair, had become a Che Guevara of sorts, leading a revolution over school reform and neighborhood control. The Amigos Charter Academy opened in the backyard of the community's Catholic church. An escape to freedom had been won.

The escape to freedom is always exhilarating, for grassroots founders of charter schools as well as the wider circle of public school critics and advocates for school choice who believe that the only way to fix government is to de-center it, disassembling the stultifying elements of bureaucracy. In addition, building a warm, nurturing community within these human-scale schools is quite rewarding.

Charter school proponents believe that education is not just a matter for the politicians and professionals; it is a matter for all of us. When we work together, we can do it. We can meet the needs of all students and enable all students to learn successfully.

Picture the following scenario: The people sitting in Pam and Tony's living room, on a frigid below-zero night, don't look like relics from the 19th century. The founding parents of a proposed charter school seem altogether normal. Among the group of 17 parents hoping to start a new charter school are soccer moms and a mechanical engineer, a karate instructor and a corporate attorney, a mutual fund manager and a musician, a welfare mom and a software computer whiz. Some have college degrees, several have no degrees past high school. One dropped out. They all have a common thread: they have lost hope that the traditional public schools can help/teach their children. They want no funky-order learning theory, no gibberish about "high-order learning skills," no "whole math" that doesn't use numbers, and no reading without phonics. "We want student results, student-centered classrooms, and academic achievement."

In the United States, a charter school is a school that is created via a legal charter. Usually they are created with an express purpose or philosophy. Typically, they are controlled in-house and not controlled by the local school district.

Charter schools are an American educational reform that allows publicly funded schools to act and operate like private schools. The theory is that competition from these schools will force the other public schools to perform better.

Critics of charter schools claim they siphon off the best students and leave the public schools worse off. Opinions vary as to the success of charter schools, in part, because of the philosophical outlook taken, and in part because charter schools vary one from the other in quality, competence, and effectiveness.

Charter schools are freed of any restrictive rules and regulations. In return, these schools are expected to achieve educational outcomes within a certain period of time (usually 3 to 5 years) or have their charters revoked by sponsors (a local school board, state educational agency, college or university, and in some areas, a nonprofit organization).

Charter schools, independently operated public schools of choice, have existed in the United States since the first charter school opened in Minnesota in 1991. Can they really boost student achievement, drive educational innovation, and develop a new model of accountability for public schools?

Enthusiasts and opponents often depict charter schools as a revolutionary change, a policy earthquake, and an unprecedented and heretofore unimaginable innovation. Boosters seize on such colorful rhetoric because it dramatizes the historic significance of their crusade. Enemies deploy the same terminology for the opposite purpose: to slow this movements' spread by portraying it as radical, risky, and unproven. Both groups tend to stand too close to the fire. Viewed from a few inches away, charter schools do represent sharp changes in the customary practices of today's large public school systems.

Some members of the public are dissatisfied with educational quality and school district bureaucracies. Today's charter initiatives are rooted in the educational reforms of the 1980s and 1990s from state mandates to improve instruction, to school-based management, school restructuring, and private/public choice initiatives.

The charter approach uses market principles while insisting that schools be nonsectarian and democratic. Many people, such as former president Bill Clinton, see charter schools, with their emphasis on autonomy and accountability, as a workable political compromise and an alternative to vouchers. Others, such as President George W. Bush, see charter schools as a way to improve schools without antagonizing the teachers' union. Charter schools are a major part of the No Child Left Behind Act.

Charter schools embody three familiar and time-trusted features of American education: they are rooted in their communities, they have cousins in the K–12 family (lab schools, magnet schools, site-managed schools, and special-focus schools), and they reveal institutional innovation and adaptation, a classic American response to a problem or opportunity.

Where did charter schools come from? Most experts agree that the phrase was first used by the late Albert Shanker, longtime president of the American Federation of Teachers, in a 1988 speech to the National Press Club and in a subsequent magazine article. He contemplated an arrangement that would enable any school or any group of teachers within a school to develop a proposal for how they could better educate children and then give them a "charter" to implement the proposal. Shanker was echoed in a 1989 article called "Education by Charter" by Ray Budde. Jumping on the bandwagon, a Minnesota legislator named Ember Reichgott Junge launched this idea in her state. By 1991, Minnesota had enacted the nation's first charter law. Several states immediately followed suit and by 1999 charter schools were up and running nationwide.

Charter schools are shaped not only by those establishing the school but also by the legislation that establishes the parameters for charter schools. The laws cover seven legal areas: charter development (how charters are granted), school status (how the school is legally defined and governance issues), fiscal (funding), students (enrollment, racial balance, civil rights, and special education), staffing and labor relations, instruction, and accountability.

The intention of most charter school legislation is to increase opportunities for learning and access to quality education for all students, to create choice for parents and students within the public school system, to provide a system of accountability for results, to encourage innovative teaching practices, to create new professional opportunities for teachers, and to encourage community and parent involvement.

What are the core features of a charter school? Let's define the beast. These schools are often described as publicly funded independent schools. Charter school founders, after approval, can operate semiautonomously from their state's education code and regulatory strings for 3 to 20 years. The basic level of per-pupil spending allocated to regular public schools is also allocated to charter schools.

A local school district, state education board, private nonprofit, or college/university can sponsor a charter school, depending on state legislation. This allows parents, community advocates, or clusters of educators and corporate entrepreneurs to craft an entirely new school. The theory of action underlying charter schools is that they will be more innovative, effective, and accountable than bureaucratically managed district schools. Charters are to be revisited and reviewed periodically, and evidence of effectiveness is allegedly put forward. Since charter schools are directly accountable to their students and parents, be they working-class Latinos, Evangelical Christians, or affluent whites, the assumption is that their directors and teachers will be responsive and innovative in advancing preferred ways of raising the academic bar and teaching children.

Some educators say that, rooted in the alternative school movement of the 1960s, and profiting from the subsequent enthusiasm over school-level control as manifested in Chicago and the small schools of New York City, the charter mechanism was first shaped by the Minnesota legislation in 1991. This legislation came on the heels of the Philadelphia movement of the late 1980s when the Philadelphia School District started a number of schools-within-schools and called them "charter." Some of them were schools of choice. Minnesota further refined the concept and developed schools according to three basic values: opportunity, choice, and responsibility for results.

Charter schools remain one of the fastest growing innovations in educational policy, enjoying broad bipartisan support from governors, state legislators, and past and present secretaries of education.

What's striking about many charter school founders is that they are dedicated to so much more than simply raising children's test scores. They talk about how kids should be raised, the cultural content of the curriculum, and the democratic or authoritative ways in which teachers relate to parents. At the charter movement's heart is a variegated set of small murals, advancing particular ways of embodying schooling within ethnic, religious, and class-based forms of child rearing. Grassroots advocates and charter directors speak of inventing new communities for learning and socialization.

Parents and teachers choose charter schools primarily for educational reasons, high academic standards, small class size, innovative approaches, or educational philosophies in line with their own. Charters are accountable for both academic results and fiscal practices to several groups, such as the sponsor that supports them, the parents who choose them, and the public that funds them.

Charter schools have become popular because many people believe that they can provide a high-quality education to public school students without the regulatory constraints imposed on conventional public schools. Urban areas are particularly fertile ground for the development of charter schools because there is a need to find ways to improve education in the face of poor resources and overcrowding in the public schools.

The goal of most charters is to provide exciting and challenging instruction that is personalized for each student. They seek to offer a clear-cut alternative to traditional public schools.

Some charters have a theme that either governs curriculum and instruction or determines the nature of their student body. Examples of this are elementary and secondary education that is trilingual/tricultural or cyberspace or technology based or a school that welcomes returned dropouts. Charters also frequently employ instructional methods such as multiage student grouping, cooperative learning, and portfolio assessment.

Many charters are created by parents who determine the curriculum and instructional practices. And, parent involvement is ongoing. They often suggest parent-children activities and homework assignments that require parent participation.

California charters use contracts to require certain parent behavior, especially their presence at the school. Other clauses include student attendance requirements, commitment to provide materials at home, and support of school codes.

Charters offer teachers unique opportunities to become directly involved in all phases of their operations, and to become school "owners" instead of simply employees.

What do charter schools look like? It is difficult to put your finger on a "typical" charter school, but policy makers and educators want to judge them as a group of schools sharing basic organizational features. In a deeper way, educators and policy wonks should be learning about what is inside charter schools that engage parents and boost student achievement and motivation, but the first questions are about how the basic contours of charters compare to conventional public schools.

For those who conceived of charter schools, the goal is to improve student achievement by fostering innovation, which occurs because the charter school is free from the rules and regulations that pertain to traditional public schools. The organizers of charter schools are motivated by the opportunity to realize an educational vision without the "red tape" involved in the traditional public schools. These schools often use a particular approach to teaching and learning (multiaged, back to basics, work oriented, special needs, etc.). Imagine a back-to-basics elementary school or a multiaged elementary school, or a high school in which students perform academic tasks and demonstrate competence before a panel of peers, parents, teachers, and community leaders. Schools may also offer day care, parenting classes, or a real-world curriculum. They also may serve a population that is not well served in the traditional school system (unwed parents, underachieving students, non-English speakers, deaf or blind students, dropouts, etc.). In one school, students meet 4 days a week, but the teachers must meet for 5. On that 5th day teachers meet, plan, and learn.

Charters are quite small. Many have a student population of 150 to 200. About two-thirds of all charter schools focus on middle or secondary grade levels. The remaining third are primary schools. This may reflect parents' greater disaffection with large, impersonal high schools, relative to their smaller neighborhood elementary schools. Many charter schools are serving a diverse range of students (Latino, African American, Hmong, American Indian, Somalian, and other African immigrants). Parents are enthused and support continues to rise.

Although some parents are also the organizers of charter schools, most are interested because they see an opportunity to send their children to a school that is more aligned with their philosophical beliefs and values than is the traditional public school. They may want a school that is smaller or one that they feel is safer. Many parents are attracted to the opportunity to be more involved in the day-to-day operation, either in management or in the classroom. Involvement extends beyond bake sales and the annual parent-night participation. Parents may be asked to contribute time and effort as lunchroom or classroom aides, playground assistants, office assistants, or direct a homework help line. Choosing a charter school, rather than having the district assign a school, can be the first step in a parent's involvement in his or her child's education.

Charter schools, unlike traditional public schools, are academically accountable on two counts. First, they must declare at the onset what their academic goals are. In order for their charter to be granted, the charter governing board must determine that those goals are rigorous and can be objectively assessed. In order for the charter to be renewed, the school must meet or exceed these goals. They cannot open their doors unless the goals are approved and they cannot remain open unless their goals are met.

The goals for charter schools can only be outlines in the most general sense. Because charter schools are given a high degree of autonomy and latitude to define their goals, these goals run the gamut from raising test scores for at-risk students to providing an agrarian-focused curriculum that promotes community building.

Despite the broad range of goals for each school, there are several key elements of success that emerge from schools that are managing to meet and even exceed their goals. Most successful charter schools:

- Remain accountable to the charter-authorizing group by meeting the goals they have outlined for themselves in their charter.
- Garner support strategically for the charter beyond the core group that is starting the school among the larger community, parents, school board, district, and support services.
- Avoid conflicts with other education entities.
- Rally a sufficiently strong contingent of supporters so that the charter effort becomes a unifying effort for a community.
- Mind the size of the school. Average enrollment for charters is approximately 150 students.
- Build on the core strength of parental satisfaction. Parent surveys have found that the majority of parents who send their children to charter schools find the charter school to be better than their former schools. Satisfaction is high.

Parents in charter schools have few risks and so much to gain. They can "walk" anytime they wish and return to the traditional public school or exercise the private school option if they have the financial means.

To keep families, charter school leadership and staff work hard to satisfy them.

Do children learn more, or differently, in charter schools? At first glance, the ability of charter schools to boost children's learning curve, relative to the growth of students in neighborhood schools, appears to be encouraging. Community Day Charter School, outside Boston, has displayed impressive achievement gains. In one academic year, the children advanced one and one-half grade levels. In Los Angeles an evaluation team claimed that two charters, Fenton and Vaughn schools, were able to move students' learning upward at rates significantly higher than comparison district schools serving similar students.

One Los Angeles charter school, Edutrain, educates troubled and homeless teens. Because Edutrain students deal with problems such as drugs, alcohol, gangs, and crime, class hours are flexible, child care is provided, and courses offer practical information that can be applied to daily life. The school was originally part of the Los Angeles School District, but after converting to charter status, Edutrain directors now set their own rules, which range from the selection of teachers hired to the number of credits students need for graduation.

One variation of charter schools, the for-profit school, may have something other than the students' education as its main interest. Some educators feel that if education is viewed as a source of profit, it may lead to a scramble to make as much money as possible and students' learning may be lost. Proponents say this is not true because they have the funds available to enhance students' academics.

Companies that operate for profit can create and manage schools independently from the public school system, or they can be hired to run troubled public schools more efficiently. The most widely publicized venture is the Edison Project.

Edison Schools is a profit-seeking organization that manages public schools under contract with local school districts or charter school authorities. The organization's goal is to offer superior education for approximately the same amount per student that districts spend in their other schools. Edison's growing popularity has stirred debate about what role nonpublic authorities should play in education funded with public tax dollars.

Edison hires its own administrators, teachers, and staff, and offers its own learning program. At Edison schools, both the school day and the school year are significantly longer than the national average. Students attending Edison schools generally have the same mix of abilities, ethnic backgrounds, and family income levels as the students in the rest of the district.

Edison Schools offers a comprehensive curriculum for kindergarten through grade 12. This curriculum stresses fundamentals of reading and mathematics for kindergarten through second grade. Emphasis on problem solving, thinking, and writing increases as students mature. Edison also focuses on technology as a learning resource and a communication tool. The project uses narrative report cards, cumulative portfolios, and other nontraditional measures of student progress.

Media entrepreneur Chris Whittle founded the Edison Project in 1991, the year the nation's first charter school law was passed. It was named for American inventor Thomas Edison to highlight the organization's commitment to inventiveness and technical creativity. Whittle assembled a team of experts in education, social service, and technology who spent 3 years developing the curriculum. The project opened its first schools in 1995. It changed its name to Edison Schools in 1999. In 2002, Edison took over the management of 20 public schools in Philadelphia. It has since spread nationwide.

Charter school successes abound. The nation's first charter school, a public school that accepts greater freedom from bureaucracy in exchange for a promise to perform at or above local standards, opened its doors in Minnesota in 1992. Since then, the movement has spawned some exciting success stories, particularly in urban areas, where such stories were badly needed. High-profile charters moved into low-income neighborhoods and proved they could take the same kids, and with less public money, and produce better results.

In suburban and more affluent areas, some charters have made less of a dent in standardized test scores, but they still achieved major gains in terms of parent satisfaction.

As stated earlier, some charter schools are conservative, back-to-basics academies, heavy on discipline, character education, and learning by drill. Others are arts-focused instructional centers, designed to appeal to creative teens who prefer a potter's wheel to an algebra textbook. Still others adopt a theme curriculum such as an Afro-centric blend of

Swahili and drumming or American Indian dancing and singing, alongside spelling and multiplication.

The charter school concept invites and allows for innovation, and successful charter schools can be found across America.

Bronx Prep (which started in 2000 in a church rectory) relies heavily on spending more time on academics and on raising expectations. Students attend school from 7:15 a.m. to 5:15 p.m., 200 days a year, which means they receive 50% more instruction time than children in traditional public schools in New York City.

"We've proven we can do it," says a faculty member at Bronx Prep. "Every time a charter school accepts students who lag behind the average academically, and then turn their performance around, that school makes the case that the problem is not the kids."

Academy of the Pacific Rim, Boston, Massachusetts, has a challenging curriculum that seeks to combine the best of Eastern education and tradition (discipline and character building) with the best of Western learning and culture (individualism and creativity). All students must study Mandarin Chinese and Tai Chi and read a play by Shakespeare every year. The school's test scores are among the highest in the Boston Public Schools.

New School for the Arts, Tempe, Arizona, has a combination of a college-preparatory curriculum with serious arts training. Graduates have gone on to some of the country's most prestigious arts schools, as well as Ivy League universities.

Minnesota New Country School, Henderson, Minnesota, is located in a small farming community 60 miles southwest of Minneapolis. It is a charter school that serves grades 7–12 from a 10-district area. There are no courses. Learning is self-directed with a heavy emphasis on communication, technology, and service learning. The Bill and Melinda Gates Foundation was so impressed by this school, its students, and its learning philosophy that it offered a $4.5 million grant to help create 15 similar schools.

The Met, located in Providence, Rhode Island, is a high school with a majority of students who dropped out of or had been expelled from local public schools. Students spend most of their weeks with an adult mentor in work-based internships of their choice. Met teachers, students, mentors, and family members work together to create personalized learning plans for each student and use comprehensive, performance-based assessment tools to measure students' achievement. Every student who has graduated has applied to and been accepted at a postsecondary institution.

North Star Academy, Newark, New Jersey, sets a shining example for schools across the nation. North Star has a challenging curriculum that incorporates an eclectic mix of educational philosophies. Students start each day with a character-building community meeting, pledge to live by core values, and must apologize publicly when they transgress these values or are late to school. Discipline is strict and consistent. Students discover the world beyond the city, such as canoeing in the Pine Barrens, hiking the Appalachian Trail, or exploring the Everglades. The school year lasts for 11 months, September to July, and students are in classes an hour longer than their district peers. In July students attend class in the mornings and teachers spend the afternoons sharpening their own skills. On state tests, North Star students score twice the district average in language arts and almost triple the average in math.

One parent said, "North Star is the best thing that has come into our lives as far as education is concerned. My son shows a lot more interest in school and he plans for the future."

Newcomers High School Academy for New Americans, Long Island City, New York, is a port of entry for immigrants into the American educational system. Over half of the students come from Ecuador, Colombia, and China. Newcomers's goal is to move students quickly into regular neighborhood schools with English-speaking students. The students receive 9 hours a week of instruction in English as a second language. The remaining time is spent in bilingual classes in Spanish and Chinese. The school offers advanced placement classes in calculus, Spanish literature, and French. Ninety percent of the graduates go on to college.

One student says, "This school treats us like a person, not a number. It is a place you feel comfortable in a new land."

High Tech High is a charter school in San Diego, California. Innovative features of the educational program include a project-based curriculum, tight linkages to the high-tech workplace, student use and understanding of information technology, strong and varied adult relationships, (advisers at the school and industry mentors), and seminars. Students from diverse backgrounds and differing skill levels work together in small groups. The school facility design offers expansive student workstations and project space to encourage both collaborative learning and individual exploration.

Francis Parker Charter School serves students from more than 30 suburban communities in north central Massachusetts. The school's philosophy is to teach all students to use their minds well. This means developing intellectual skills in a few essential areas, such as writing, reading, and mathematics through exploration of "essential questions" that cross disciplinary lines. Students must complete various demonstrations of mastery and portfolio requirements in order to graduate.

Oh Day Aki Charter School, Minneapolis, Minnesota, is a charter school that has 95% American Indian students enrolled in kindergarten through 12th grade. The school's mission is to enhance the lives of society's most needy members, many of whom are the children, and to develop with them the skills which will enable them to maintain independence in society and to be successful, contributing members of society. The intent is to make a lasting impact on the children and adults enrolled in the school. Oh Day Aki was started in 1972 to meet the needs of American Indian students not adequately met in mainstream public education. Initially funded by federal grants and later as a Minneapolis alternative school, Oh Day Aki became a charter school in the spring of 1999. The school is sponsored by the Minneapolis Public Schools and currently has 245 students enrolled who are benefiting from the small school environment, with small class sizes and a "hands-on" learning curriculum. The school's program is empirically and culturally based, emphasizes family commitment to education, and seeks to resolve family social service issues that are negatively affecting the students' educational success.

These are schools of choice. Both teachers and families are associated with the schools because they choose to be.

Charter schools are steadily growing schools in high demand. While not every public school is a sinking ship, charter schools have offered a life ring to many students who are floundering in their traditional school setting. Whether through the implementation of new best practices like Core Knowledge or Community-based Learning, or a return to the tried-and-true methods like Direct Instruction and Conduct Codes, charter schools are succeeding with students and achieving high levels of satisfaction and involvement from parents. Teachers are flocking to charters in order to develop their own professional potential and to improve the educational process.

Charters allow for immediate implementation of successful curriculum, innovative policies, and rigorous academics. They allow for swifter eradication of those pedagogical policy or management systems that are not working. Charters have been known to eliminate the achievement gap, motivate students, engage parents, develop community partners, and provide responsible management.

Ultimately, the measure of success for charter schools is not the boards or lack of boundary lines, or their innovation, but the education of their students.

Overall, charter schools are:

- open to all students
- pioneers and innovators in public education
- meeting parents needs and developing an understanding of how parents should be involved in both school and at home
- appealing places to work for staff
- empowering teachers
- committed to improving public education
- operated by an exciting mixture of leaders
- playing an important role in school reform
- demonstrating a record of student achievement
- somewhat more racially diverse, balancing diversity with democratic discourse
- pursuing an educational vision and mission
- havens for students who have had unsuccessful educational experiences elsewhere

During the past 20 years, segments of the American public have expressed growing dissatisfaction with public education. The belief that education is failing many of our children has led to an exhaustive array of initiatives, mandates, and movements designed to improve educational offerings. All of these initiatives have taken place within the context of the traditional public schools structure operated by federal, state, and local governing bodies.

Many frustrated teachers, parents, and other stakeholders believe that government is not in a position to provide solutions to improve education because the traditional government structures and mandates are a large part of the problem. One solution is to reinvent the system by which we provide and run public education, a reinvented system of choice, flexibility, and accountability that includes the creation of charter schools. Communities are invited to create new public schools with high levels of autonomy and to be innovative in ways that may or may not embrace traditional educational structures. These schools are invited to take new and unchartered paths, but also are held responsible for ensuring their paths lead to academic success for students.

Charter schools introduce a line of thinking that is foreign to many in education. The basic premise is that, given the opportunity to choose a different school for their children, many parents will choose to leave the traditional public school in favor of a charter school that offers unique philosophy, culture, curriculum, or organizational style better suited to meet the educational needs of their children.

The charter model introduces the theory of market forces into public education. Both traditional public schools and charter schools are forced to be responsive to parents or risk losing their students and the tax dollars that come with these students. Charters have the added burden of not only attracting students but also keeping them by satisfying their educational goals.

The structural inequalities that mark American society and erode the hopes of so many children often are ignored by school reformers. Middle-class parents invest heavily in education, reading to their toddlers, moving to communities with "good" schools, and watching after their child's homework. For these parents, education has delivered economic returns and social openings. They pass on this faith in formal schooling to their children through specific practices inside the home. But for parents who work swing shifts, who face violence and intimidation in their urban neighborhoods, or who can't afford to move to quiet suburbs and better schools, tinkering with local governance of schooling may have only a marginal effect on their child's achievement.

Charter schools, like other forms of school choice, allow eager parents in blue-collar and low-income communities to escape what they see as lousy schools. We must always offer options for parents who go up against long odds to improve their children's lives. Charter schools can become an effective part of the solution.

There is no "one best reform" strategy and perhaps none will emerge. This is a big, diverse nation, and our children's education is too important to give any single idea a monopoly. But, to many, charter schools seem to be the most vibrant force in education today, not only because of their broad appeal and their roots in the principle of public education, but also because they are themselves so diverse. Charters are public schools that invite a thousand innovations and move us toward a powerful new framework of educational accountability. Perhaps most heartening, charter schools are providing a worthy alternative to conventional district schools for those who need it most, families whose children are stuck in failing schools.

5

MAGNET SCHOOLS: THE STUFF OF KIDS' DREAMS

Nothing, not all the armies in the world, can stop an idea whose time has come.

—Victor Hugo

Cheyenne was ready to drop out of school in his ninth-grade year. "I hated the daily grind and the b.s. I would come home thinking I'd spent six hours in classes and I could have gotten all the stuff we did done in an hour. Half of the day was spent taking attendance, listening to teachers try to discipline other kids, and listening to endless talking, lectures with no discussion. The attitudes of both the kids and the teachers towards one another sucked."

As a last resort, a school social worker suggested that Cheyenne apply for entrance to the American Indian Magnet School, located within a local high school in the district. Cheyenne applied and was accepted. His life changed. "Remember the saying, 'tell me, I forget, show me, I remember, involve me, I understand,' well, it's true. The teachers involved me, made me feel welcome, really cared. They understood me, they challenged me." Cheyenne graduated from the American Indian Magnet School in June 2006. He is currently enrolled at the University of Minnesota and hopes to become a teacher.

One of the most popular options in school choice is the magnet school. Magnet schools may be self-contained facilities or schools within schools, part of other school campuses. They are created with the purpose of drawing bright and highly motivated students to their programs. As alternatives to more traditional schools, they are attractive because teachers and students work together in small groups and thus have opportunities to share common interests and experiment with nontraditional learning techniques.

In many magnet schools, the curriculum is specialized. A large number of the several thousand magnets across the country concentrate on math, science, foreign language, or the arts. But there are exceptions. The Center for International Commerce in Long Beach, California, prepares high school graduates for careers in international relations and global business. City Magnet in Lowell, Massachusetts, teaches traditional classes every morning, then allows students to manage and take part in a society of their own creation every afternoon. During that time they learn math by working and paying taxes (using play money), study law by carrying out mock trials, and learn about politics by holding class elections.

Magnet schools are open to students of all races and economic levels, and thus can be avenues to success for culturally diverse students. Some magnets, such as the Environmental Technology Academy in Philadelphia, Pennsylvania, emphasize vocational skills and attract hardworking students who want to attend daily and reap the benefits of working at jobs available in the community.

In magnet schools, attendance is high, often above 96%. Magnets graduate more than their share of National Merit Scholarship winners, and state mandated test scores are exceptional. Educators have also found that the presence of a magnet program on a traditional campus can produce a halo effect, encouraging students in traditional classes to perform better (Yancey, 1995).

Magnet schools gained prominence in the 1970s as a tool for achieving voluntary desegregation in lieu of forced busing. An early study of magnet schools sponsored by the U.S. Department of Education (1974) found that magnet schools were developed first in large urban school districts seeking to reduce racial isolation in their schools through voluntary means rather than mandatory student assignment. Magnets were intended to provide incentives for parents to remain in the public school system and to send their children to integrated schools or neighborhoods to encourage students of other races to enroll in these schools. The educational programs at these magnet schools were modeled on well-established specialty schools that offered advanced programs to selected students, such as Bronx School of Science, Boston Latin School, and Lane Tech in Chicago. Early magnet school curricular programs mirrored specialty school themes such as the previously mentioned math and science as well as the performing arts. However, magnet school programs were designed to be different in one very important way: magnet school enrollment was driven by student choice based on interest rather than selection of students by testing.

Some 35 years later, many districts continue to utilize magnet schools to reduce minority group isolation; however, in the intervening years, the purposes of magnet schools have continued to evolve and expand. When the federal Magnet Schools Assistance Program was first authorized in 1985, its intent was two-fold: reduce, eliminate, or prevent minority group isolation and provide instruction that would substantially strengthen students' knowledge and skills. Subsequently, expectations for magnet schools have broadened. Today, school districts are using them to accomplish a range of important and related purposes: enhancing student learning and narrowing the achievement gap, giving public school parents more choice in their child's educational experience, and incubating innovative educational methods and practices that can raise the bar for all schools.

The demands of a rapidly changing society and increasing pressure for educational reform (coupled with a rise in absenteeism, dropout rates, and academic failure in traditional schools) have lead to the creation of several thousand magnet schools in urban school districts across the country. In order to facilitate the transition to a multicultural community and meet the prevailing desire for academic excellence, magnets have adopted innovative educational practices as an enticement for students and their families. Magnets are also appealing to districts with schools in need of improvement under the federal No Child Left Behind Act, which specifically acknowledges their value for the purposes stated earlier.

As parents' voices grow louder with dissatisfaction of the public school system as it exists today, government concerns have taken steps to "reinvent the wheel" so to speak. Magnet schools are an option that has been presented.

The U.S. Department of Education's (1974) definition is as follows: "The term *magnet school* means a public elementary school, public secondary school, public elementary education center, or public secondary center that offers a special curriculum capable of attracting substantial numbers of students of different cultural/racial backgrounds."

The theory behind magnet schools as a desegregation tool is simple: Create a school so distinctive and appealing, so magnetic that it will draw a diverse range of families from throughout the community eager to enroll their children even if it means having them bused to a different neighborhood. To do this, the school must offer an educational option or specialty that is not available in other area schools.

Early magnet school research (Oakes, 1985) identified five common magnet school themes: the fine, applied, or performing arts; the sciences; social studies occupations; general academics; and traditional and fundamental schools. But a look across district magnet programs today reveals a much wider variety of curricular specialties and educational approaches, reflecting the interests and resources of their communities. Today you will find aerospace education, communications, culinary arts, environmental science, international studies, video and sound production, International Baccalaureate, language immersion, law enforcement, military science, Montessori, and Paideia.

What is distinctive about magnet schools? Three distinguishing characteristics come to mind:

1. Magnets provide a distinctive curriculum or instructional approach.
2. Magnets attract students from outside an assigned neighborhood attendance zone.
3. Magnets have diversity as an explicit purpose.

Magnet schools also have three goals:

1. Promote and maintain diversity.
2. Provide a unique or specialized curriculum or educational approach. Creating supportive, personal environments while

placing high expectations on student potential and progress attracts students.
3. Improve achievement for all students participating in the magnet program.

Parents, students, and community members assess the needs of their school district and design a specific magnet program to serve these needs.

Who attends magnet schools? While magnet schools are more racially balanced than their traditional counterparts, students who attend magnet schools are less likely to be eligible for free or reduced lunch programs and are more likely to live in two-parent households, with parents who are employed and have earned some type of postsecondary degree, as compared with students who don't attend magnet schools. These findings apply to the white, African American, and Latino students who attend magnet schools. However, this is changing in some areas of the country. In Jacksonville, Florida, magnet schools have attracted about 20,000 students who come from primarily single-parent families and qualify for free or reduced lunches.

What are the achievement levels of students who attend magnet schools as compared to students at nonmagnet schools? For the most part, research shows that the achievement levels of students who attend magnet schools are greater than the achievement levels of students who attend traditional schools. Students in magnet schools significantly outperformed their peers attending nonmagnets in social studies, science, and reading. Also many students at magnet schools achieve higher scores on state assessments in math, reading, science, and social studies than a comparable sample of students in neighborhood schools (Steel & Levine, 2004).

What are some methods magnets use to meet their objectives? Many magnet schools adopt cooperative learning activities and encourage small group discussion. Extracurricular activities and special projects provide opportunities for students to share diverse skills, and multicultural lessons are regularly introduced into the curriculum. With an emphasis on mutual respect and appreciation and examples of positive interracial relations set by the staff, a general atmosphere of trust and goodwill is nurtured among all members of the school community.

Student evaluations are based on progress and effort as well as achievement and may be written as comments rather than grades, thus diffusing competition, lessening the tendency to stereotype or create hierarchies among students, and avoiding the sense of failure those in the bottom half of traditional grading systems tend to feel. Instead, students are judged by their capacity to better their last performance and fulfill their own preestablished goals.

From individually guided education to back-to-basics techniques, magnets appeal to student interest across race, age, class, and achievement levels by offering challenging courses that focus on special themes and by using approaches that match individual cognitive skills. Teachers have the opportunity to circulate in classes and attend to the specific learning needs of each student. Generally, small and flexible magnets change curriculum to meet student needs and depend on a resourceful, dedicated staff and supportive community.

How can magnets meet their specific challenges? Magnets are appearing attractive but not elitist by appealing to interest rather than ability. They are appearing diverse but not second-rate by providing sound criteria and objectives. They are developing in students both the ability to work cooperatively with persons of different backgrounds and skills and the ability to take responsibility for their own progress in learning. Magnets are responding to constituent needs, welcoming parent, community, teacher, and student input in design and direction. Magnets also make special efforts to encourage participation by the most marginalized and disadvantaged populations. Finally, leadership that is strong without disempowering its staff guides magnet schools' innovative style. Magnets are not temporary or experimental, but are participating in mutually beneficial relationships with traditional schools.

KEY QUESTIONS TO ASK WHEN SEARCHING FOR A MAGNET SCHOOL

Parent access to information is a critical variable in achieving diversity in and across magnet schools. The more aware parents are of options, the more likely they are to pursue them. Schools that "scream their theme" will be able to recruit parents.

Here are some of the key questions to ask when considering a magnet school:

- What is the school's mission or educational philosophy?
- How is the school's magnet theme incorporated into the school environment?
- How does this school encourage and monitor students' progress toward meeting graduation standards?
- Do the students work in small groups on various tasks or spend most of their time in large group instruction?
- What is the school's approach to student discipline and safety?
- What are some highlights of the reading and math curriculum?
- What are the resources available to students?
- How is technology used to support teaching and learning at this school?
- Are community partners involved in the school?
- What materials are available in the classrooms to support learning (visual tools, hands-on tools, technological tools)?
- Are there opportunities for different grade levels to interact with supervision (reading buddies, etc.)?
- Is there an after-school enrichment program?
- How does this school support students who have academic, social, or emotional needs?

One type of magnet that is of note is focus schools. Lately, a number of school districts, especially in urban areas, have been establishing focus schools, which is often considered as an enhancement of the magnet school. These institutions have a specific theme and are targeted for particular students. In 1990, this concept of focus schools received a strong boost from a RAND Corporation study suggesting that special purpose schools would probably be preferable to comprehensive high school for most students in New York City (Hill, Foster, & Gendler, 1990). The study calls such schools "high schools with character," those that have a clear, coherent commitment to character, as well as academic development; feature a core of shared learning; emphasize the reciprocal responsibilities of the school's students and adults; and stress achievement. The ability of the school's focus to attract both students and staff, and to provide a framework for an effective educational program is the key to success of focus schools. The focus enhances a school's academic effectiveness and promotes equity. It attracts students and staff who share an interest in a specific instructional program. Focus school advocates suggest that student interests and family priorities may offer far more practical guidance for developing programs and grouping students than do ability levels. There is no longer reason to believe that what average, or even poor, students need instructionally is very different from what the ablest need. There is little reason to believe that just because one child is as bright as another that the two hold any interests in common. Thus, shared interest in drama, technology, or mathematics may well drive an effective curriculum for a group of students regardless of their diverse abilities.

A theme or focus must possess logical coherence. A shared set of assumptions and values and acceptance of the resulting practices can bring coherence to the school's program and thus motivate students to apply themselves to it.

Of the several thousand magnet schools across the country, four stand out as having creative and innovative programs. These are successful magnet programs and the districts they are located in are in support of what is happening.

Duval County Public Schools, serving Jacksonville, Florida, has been home to two unique magnet high schools since the early 1980s. Duval's magnet schools are schools-within-a-school magnets and create an environment in which students can excel by choosing what best meets their needs. The program is diverse and academically focused. Frank H. Peterson Academy of Technology graduates students with both a diploma and a license in a particular vocational area. Andrew Jackson Medical Professions and Criminal Justice High School enrolls mainly African American students from low-income families. The graduates proceed directly into the workforce. Achievement scores have risen in the district and there is a waiting list to enroll. This district says that their success is due to open lines of communication between parents, administrators, and staff; research themes; strong leaders; and "screaming your theme."

After the Hamilton County School System and the Chattanooga, Tennessee, City School System merged in 1997, the superintendent of the newly combined district championed the creation of magnet schools to reduce, eliminate, and prevent minority group isolation within the schools. Hamilton requires parents whose child attends a magnet school to volunteer a minimum of 18 hours a year at their school and has also developed several successful community partnerships, which provide funding and resources. Most schools have typical themes such as math and science, performing arts, and technology, but several magnets are organized around specific pedagogies, such as the two Paideia schools, which use unique approaches to student learning, including a focus on seminar discussions and coaching of academic skills. Hamilton County Schools offers an example of how magnets are sometimes used to serve multiple goals. Coinciding with and in support of a city-driven, urban-renewal effort, the district built two magnet high schools in low-income neighborhoods of color adjacent to Chattanooga's downtown business center and converted two older downtown neighborhood schools into magnets.

Like many districts serving urban areas, Hamilton had been steadily losing students to local parochial and private schools and to the surrounding suburbs. Its downtown magnet themes were conceived to recapture some of these students. Two of the magnet schools are museum schools (grades K–5 and grades 6–8) that work closely with the area's seven museums. Of the other two, one focuses on classical studies (literature, art, history, architecture, and music) and the other bases its instruction on Howard Gardner's theory of multiple intelligences. Hamilton attributes its success to the right personnel, a focus on professional development, marketing, and learning from other magnets.

Hot Springs, Arkansas, School District is an all-magnet district; its only nonmagnet schools are alternative schools serving court-involved or emotionally challenged youth. Its program began in 2000 after a federal district court ordered it as part of a multidistrict desegregation plan. Arkansas law says that students may attend school in other districts if their transfer will improve racial integration. Hot Springs' magnet program serves students from 12 other districts as well as their own district.

Hot Springs now has four magnet elementary schools, one magnet middle school, and one magnet high school. The magnet themes are aligned vertically from the elementary level to the high school level (where they are called career academies). Within these themes are various strands across several grade levels. While the themes are essential, the instructional focus is driven by state academic standards and stresses mathematics and literacy. Hot Springs attributes its success to the use of data, choice of themes, research, use of outside expertise, and the all-magnet approach.

In 1975 Houston, Texas, Independent School District received a court order to desegregate and decided early on to use a magnet program as its tool for desegregation. In the 1975–1976 school year, Houston opened 32 magnet schools. By 1980, the court mandate for desegregation was ended, and magnets became an integral part of educational enrichment for both urban and suburban students.

Houston now supports 54 magnet elementary schools, 28 magnet middle schools, and 27 magnet high schools. The objectives are twofold: to provide academic programs whose quality and special focus will attract students from across the district and to increase the percentage of students attending integrated schools.

DeBakey High School for Health Professions, located in the renowned Texas Medical Center, is an example of a magnet with a unique theme strong enough to attract students from all over the huge district. The school provides a rigorous and comprehensive precollege program for students pursuing careers in medicine, health care, and the sciences. Houston attributes its success with magnets to regular meetings with all magnet administrators, commitment from top levels at the district, formal policies and procedures, and a rich variety of choices.

When magnet schools began more than 30 years ago, these schools provided an enormous breakthrough for public education: racially integrated schools coupled with the concept of school choice. Today, parents continue to choose what kinds of schools they'd like, what special signatures or themes (computers, arts, etc.) or pedagogical approaches (back to basics, Montessori, etc.) are popular. One magnet district has labeled their magnet programs as "work-site" schools and priority is given to applicants whose parents work in the targeted area. The opportunity to have their children nearby is an added attraction for suburban commuters who like the idea of spending more time with their children as they commute and want to be involved with their children's school.

Magnet schools today are also paying greater attention to economic diversity. A number of districts from La Crosse, Wisconsin, to Raleigh,

North Carolina, to San Francisco, California, to Cambridge, Massachusetts, are relying primarily on economic indicators as a legal way of promoting both economic and racial diversity. Too often magnet schools have been racially integrated but economically segregated, composed of middle-class black, Latino, and white students, leaving the rest of the school district with a greater poverty concentration.

Magnet schools have proven themselves to be high performing. A successful magnet school has the following:

- an adequate financial base (as measured against student needs) to provide small class sizes, modern equipment, and the like
- a budget where money is spent wisely, on the classroom rather than on bureaucracy
- an orderly environment
- a stable student and teacher population with well-qualified teachers
- a meaty curriculum and high expectations
- active parental involvement
- motivated peers who value achievement and encourage it among classmates
- high-achieving peers, whose knowledge is shared informally with classmates

The unique magnet goal of attracting students away from their neighborhood attendance zone requires special effort based on careful and informal planning. Parents must be motivated to abandon their traditional role of accepting an assigned slot for their student, and instead to actively seek out information about the best choice for their child.

Appealing to choice is the key. When people choose to be somewhere, their attitude is different.

Magnet schools go beyond segregation. Not only do they promote racial and ethnic equity in public education, but they strive to promote improved teaching and learning. Their theme-based approach promotes innovation in programs and practice, staff and curricula coherence, increased parent and community involvement, and greater student engagement. This adds up to higher student achievement.

Magnet schools can also promote healthy competition among district schools. Faced with the prospect of losing students to magnets, many neighborhood schools examine the competition to understand the attraction while, at the same time, examining their own program to see how they might improve it. The superintendent of one magnet district says that the belief that "our school is as good as yours" has had a "ripple effect across the district," with traditional schools pushing themselves harder. Some adopt or adapt magnet school principles and practices to better serve their own students. As this happens, magnets, in turn, must ratchet up their own efforts to remain distinctive. Magnets are becoming part of a larger school improvement effort.

Magnets are providing quality programs that engage students in the learning process, leading to higher achievement. Because students disengage from learning long before they drop out of school, magnets provide focused programs that will keep the students engaged in learning, keep them in school, and prepare them for their future.

6

HOMESCHOOLING: TESTING OUR FREEDOM

> We need to be able to make choices for our children, and it should be the parents' choice, not the state's.
>
> —Homeschool parent

Ellen Bicheler didn't start out with homeschooling as a vision when her children were young. Instead it generated out of her daughter Melissa's negative junior high experience. She was assaulted, teased, and bored. Melissa begged to get out of her junior high school and presented her parents with a proposal for homeschooling that made so much sense that they agreed to a one-year commitment to try it.

Ellen said that the decision to homeschool was agonizing. She felt it would add extra work at a time when she wanted to pursue her own interest in freelance writing and spend more time in her garden. How ironic that homeschooling, more than anything, provided a path for her own interests to flourish. As Ellen watched Melissa pursue her interests with intensity and commitment, she realized that there were ways of doing things other than the old public school and college model she was familiar with. They were not locked into curriculums that others deemed important.

Ellen goes on to say that the transition to homeschooling has been very beneficial. After two years, she felt the family was much closer and stronger. Respect for each other had grown. The children gained freedom and independence. Lindsay, age 9, had joined the program, and Ellen had more time to write, read, and pursue gardening. They all share the housework. Their biggest challenge was, and still is, the scrutiny they received from the general public and, in particular, the neighbors. When the neighbors first asked Lindsay what she was doing for homeschooling, she would say, "Nothing." She would say this because she was no longer studying out of textbooks. They were going to the pond to study pond life. Ellen supplemented this with talks from naturalists and books from the library. The children were no longer studying a prescribed curriculum and nothing resembled a classroom.

Ellen said that the worst moment came when an elderly neighbor accused her and her husband of neglect and reported them to social services. She had left to run an errand, and while she was gone, the children had set up a lemonade stand in front of the house. They were soliciting the neighbors to buy their lemonade. The neighbor seemed to think that they should have been in the house learning their lessons.

One unexpected benefit of homeschooling came from getting away from the cultural, consumer values of the school. There is no peer pressure to have the "right" pair of jeans or the current toys. The children are thinking more for themselves and can point out unethical advertisements and politics.

Ellen's husband, Michael, added that homeschooling offers a lot of educational choices. They have had to find out what works and adjust accordingly. Melissa is very self-motivated and thrives on doing academics on her own. Lindsay likes to have her parents work with her. Both children make lists of things they want to study and do.

Ellen urges other homeschoolers to seek out support groups, friends, and homeschooling books and magazines to help them get through the process. Everyone will have different issues to work out. She also says that the key to a successful transition into homeschooling from other systems is to take it slowly and be patient with yourself and your family. Accept that there are people out there that aren't going to agree with your ideas. Ellen has learned to be flexible and discard things that do not work. She is not afraid to try new ideas. Above all, she says, parents need to let their homeschooling system evolve for them and their family (Bickler, 2005).

A growing number of parents are choosing to educate their children at home. This has become a feasible option for dedicated parents who want to ensure a quality education for their children. Reports have shown that homeschooled children score much higher than average on standardized tests and college entrance exams and also grow up to become hard-working, upstanding citizens (Barker, 2001).

Amid the sorry state of American education today are heroes who are rescuing children in a profoundly personal way. They are the homeschoolers, parents who sacrifice time and income to teach their children at home. Homeschooling is the ultimate in parental involvement.

Teaching children at home isn't for everyone and no one advocates that every parent try it. There are many good schools, many private and some public, that are doing a better job than some parents could do for their own children. But the fact is that homeschooling is working, and working surprisingly well, for the growing number of parents and children who choose it. This fact is all the more remarkable when one considers that these dedicated parents must juggle teaching with all the other demands and chores of modern life. Also, they get little or nothing back from what they pay in taxes for a public school system they do not patronize.

Parents who homeschool do so for a variety of reasons. Some want a strong moral or religious emphasis in their children's education. Others are fleeing unsafe public schools or schools where discipline and academics have taken a backseat to fuzzy "feel-good" or politically correct dogma. Many homeschool parents complain about the pervasiveness in public schools of trendy instructional methods that border on pedagogical malpractice.

Homeschool parents are fiercely protective of their constitutional right to educate their children. In early 1994, the House of Representatives voted to mandate that all teachers, including parents in the home, acquire state certification in the subjects they teach. A massive campaign of letters, phone calls, faxes, and e-mails from homeschoolers produced one of the most stunning turnabouts in legislative history: by a vote of 424 to 1, the House reversed itself and then approved an amendment that affirmed the rights and independence of homeschool parents.

Critics have long harbored a jaundiced view of parents who educate children at home. These critics argue that children need the guidance of professionals and the social interaction that comes from being in class with others. Homeschooled children, these critics say, will be socially and academically stunted by the confines of the home.

Opposition to homeschooling comes from varied sources, including teachers' unions and school districts. Opponents' stated concerns fall into several broad categories, including academic quality and completeness, loss of income for the schools, socialization of children with peers, political correctness, and fear of religious or social extremism. Opponents often argue that homeschooling parents are sheltering their children and denying them opportunities that are their children's right, while depleting the schools' income.

However, the facts suggest otherwise. A 2000 report by the National Home Education Research Institute shows that homeschooled children score in the 85th percentile or higher in math, reading, science, language, and social studies. Reports from state after state show homeschoolers scoring significantly better than the norm on college entrance examinations. Prestigious universities, including Harvard and Yale, accept homeschooled children eagerly and often.

Homeschooling (also called home education) is the education of children at home and in the community, in contrast to education in an institution such as a public or parochial school. In the United States, homeschooling is the focus of a substantial minority movement among parents who wish to provide their children with a custom or more complete education, which they feel is unattainable in most public or even private schools.

Homeschooling means different things to different people. For some families, homeschooling means duplicating school at home complete with textbooks, report cards, and regularly scheduled field trips. For others, homeschooling is simply the way they live their lives, children and adults living and learning together with a seamlessness that would challenge an observer to determine which was "home" and which was "school." If you think of a kind of homeschooling continuum, with "school at home" at one end and "learning and living completely integrated" on the other, you would find homeschoolers scattered along that line with every possible variation of what homeschooling could mean.

Homeschool parents approach their task in a variety of ways. While some discover texts and methods as they go, others plan their work well in advance, often assisted by other homeschoolers or associations that have sprung up to aid those who choose the option. Common to every homeschool parent is the belief that the education of their children is too important to hand over to someone else.

The word *homeschooling* conjures up many different images in the minds of those who contemplate doing it. Some see siblings gathered around the kitchen table where their mother reviews a list of vocabulary words prior to a test. Others envision the families they bump into at the grocery store, the community center, or the skiing slopes during the day. Still others recall the teen down the street, a serious learner accepting the responsibility for his own education and tasting what the world has to offer. All images are correct. Homeschooling has permeated mainstream consciousness as an acceptable educational alternative.

Homeschooling is an alternative means of education that has proven to be controversial in the United States. The general historic foundations of homeschooling originate with the informal education that existed in America before the rise of public schools in the late 19th and early 20th centuries. For example, famous figures such as Thomas Jefferson, Jane Austen, Abraham Lincoln, and Louisa May Alcott might be considered to have been homeschooled, as they were self-educated or had tutors while growing up, but received little formal schooling.

Graduates of home education have made numerous crucial contributions to America and the world. Some of the many prominent people of the past who were home educated for a significant period of time include: Presidents John Quincy Adams, James Buchanan, Millard Fillmore, William Henry Harrison, Andrew Johnson, James Madison, Theodore Roosevelt, Franklin Roosevelt, Zachary Taylor, George Washington, and Woodrow Wilson. First ladies include Martha Washington and Abigail Adams; others include Susan B. Anthony, Alexander Graham Bell, Pearl Buck, George Washington Carver, Agatha Christie, Winston Churchill, Charles Dickens, Thomas Edison, Albert Einstein, Benjamin Franklin, Robert Frost, Patrick Henry, Margaret Mead, Florence Nightingale, George Patton, Albert Schweitzer, Booker T. Washington, Laura Ingalls Wilder, Orville and Wilbur Wright, and modern-day tennis superstars Serena and Venus Williams.

Although estimates vary, roughly 1–2 million children are homeschooled in the United States (National Home Education Network), 90,000 in the

United Kingdom (Home Education Network/UK), and an additional 26,000 in Australia and New Zealand. Individual motivations to homeschool, homeschooling methods, and the results of homeschooling (both social and academic) are varied and are the source of vibrant debate.

Why homeschool? Proponents of home education evoke parental responsibility and the classical liberal arguments for personal freedom from government intrusion. Most homeschooling advocates are wary of the established educational institution for various reasons. Some are religious conservatives who see nonreligious education as contrary to their moral or religious systems. Others feel that they can more effectively tailor a curriculum to suit an individual student's academic strengths and weaknesses, especially those with learning disabilities. Still others feel that the negative social pressures of schools (such as bullying, drugs, crime, and other school-related problems) are detrimental to a child's proper development. And finally, some say it is a remedy for overcrowded classrooms, cookie-cutter curriculums, and indifferent teachers that plague so many schools today.

Options, which make homeschooling attractive to some families, also include:

- Parents may choose to allow their child to have a longer exploratory, play-oriented childhood, encouraging the development of a rich imagination and preacademic skills, which can foster later academic success.
- The flexibility of the education schedule allows each student to work at his or her own pace, enjoy family vacations and outings, and integrate outside activities or current events with subjects they are studying.
- Religion, ethics, and character topics not included in public school curriculums can be freely taught.
- Nontraditional curriculums and unusual subjects such as Latin and Greek can be taught.
- Geography, art, and music curriculums can be enhanced.
- Money management and business topics can be integrated with a family business.

The following are some of the advantages to adopting a homeschooling lifestyle. This is only a partial list. Any homeschooling family could come up with more items. I hope this list helps you with your decision.

- Parents are with their children all day.
- Parents know and understand their children and are more influential in their lives, even as they enter the teen years.
- Homeschooling prevents premature parent-child separation, avoiding inappropriate pressure on children.
- Children are allowed to mature at their own speeds, no "hurried-child" syndrome.
- Parents and other adults are the primary role models.
- Homeschooling provides positive and appropriate socialization with peers and adults.
- Homeschooled children are largely free from peer pressure.
- Homeschooled children are comfortable interacting with people of all ages.
- Homeschooled children view adults as an integrated part of their world and natural partners in learning.
- Family values and beliefs are central to social, academic, and emotional development.
- Family life revolves around its own needs and priorities rather than the demands of school.
- Homeschooling creates and maintains positive sibling relationships.
- Homeschooling promotes good communication and emotional closeness within a family.
- Research shows that the two most important factors in reading and overall educational success are a positive home influence and parental involvement; homeschooling provides both.
- A child's natural thirst for learning is nurtured, not squelched, and learning becomes a life-long joy.
- Each child's education can be tailored to his or her unique interests and learning style and allows time to pursue special interests.
- Homeschooling children enjoy unlimited resources; the world is the classroom, and resources abound in the community.
- Homeschooled children become independent learners and thinkers who are secure in their own convictions.

As I summarize some of the benefits of homeschooling think about the following: A wise man once said, "We can teach our children to have courage, faith, and endurance; they can teach us to laugh, to sing, and to love" (Kelp, 1997, p. 10). For many, the deepest and most abiding benefit of homeschooling is the claiming or reclaiming of their family. Homeschooling families spend incredible amounts of time together living, learning, and playing. They have the opportunity to develop a depth of understanding and a commitment to the family that is difficult to attain when family members spend their days going in separate directions. Many families enjoy the flexibility homeschooling provides both parents and children. The children can learn about things they are interested in at a time in their lives when they are ready to learn. No preconceived schedule forces them ahead or holds them back. Vacations and outings can be planned for times when the family is ready, and often when the crowds are smaller or the cost lower. Children can learn about the real world by being part of it. Children can receive a superior education attuned specifically to their needs, learning styles, personalities, and interests.

Is homeschooling legal? Yes, homeschooling is legal in all 50 states, although in many states homeschooling parents are occasionally threatened with prosecution under truancy laws. Laws and regulations may vary from school district to school district. Read the laws for your state before you begin.

For example, in Minnesota, the law states that to establish and operate a qualified home school you must teach reading, writing, literature, fine arts, math, science, history, geography, government, health, and physical education. The parents do not need a teaching license, must file a "Non-Public Compulsory Instructions Report" with the local district superintendent by October 1 of each school year, and submit quarterly reports showing achievement for each child in the required subjects. In addition, an annual standardized test must be administered and reported. California is similar but also requires parents to maintain attendance records. New York is the same but adds required attendance 180 days of the year, 900 hours per year for grades K–12, and 990 hours per year for grades 7–12. Florida has no attendance specified and no subject requirements but does require that a portfolio of records and materials (log of texts used and sample worksheets) be maintained, that standardized tests and assessments be given by a certified teacher, and that the child be evaluated by a certified teacher or a psychologist.

The U.S. Supreme Court has never ruled on homeschooling specifically, but in *Wisconsin v. Yoder*, 406 US 205 (1972), the court supported the right of Amish parents to keep their children out of public schools for religious reasons. A few school districts have extension programs, which allow homeschooled students to use district resources such as the school library or computer labs, or to meet with a teacher periodically for curriculum review and suggestions.

Is homeschooling for you? Making the decision to homeschool is usually very difficult and should not be taken lightly. It is a personal decision that I can't make for you, but maybe I can help in the thought process. When making the homeschool decision, consider the following:

- Time commitment. Homeschooling tends to take up a lot of time in your day. It is more than just sitting down with books for a couple of hours. There are experiments and projects to be done, lessons to prepare, papers to grade, field trips, park days, and music lessons, and the list goes on.
- Personal sacrifice. The homeschool parent has little personal time or time alone. Parent and child are basically together 24/7.
- Financial strain. Homeschool can be accomplished very inexpensively; however, it usually requires that the teaching parent will not be working outside of the home. Some sacrifices will be made if the family is used to two incomes.
- Socialization. More attention will need to be given to getting your children together with others. The beauty of homeschooling is being able to have more control of the social contacts your child makes.
- Household organization. Housework and laundry still have to be done, but it probably won't get done first thing in the morning. If a stickler for a spotless house, you might be in for a surprise. Not only does housework need to be let go at times, but homeschooling creates messes and clutter in itself.
- Both parents must be in agreement. In a two-parent family, it is important that both parents agree to try homeschooling. It is very difficult to homeschool if one parent is against it.

- Is your child willing? A willing student is always helpful. Ultimately, it is a decision the parent needs to make, but if your child is dead set against it, you will have a hard time of it.
- One year at a time. Homeschooling is not a lifetime commitment; most homeschool families take one year at a time.
- Intimidated by teaching? If you can read and write, you should be able to teach your children. The curriculum and teacher manuals and materials will help through the planning and teaching. Get help from others if you get stuck or hire tutors for the difficult subjects.

Are you willing to make the personal and financial sacrifices that homeschooling requires? If so, give it a year and see how it goes. Your next step is to learn how to get started.

The following are guidelines for getting started in homeschooling:

- First, make the big decision. Read as much as you can about homeschooling.
- Check out the homeschooling laws in your state or area. It is usually easy to satisfy the laws.
- Find a support group in your area. Support groups can help you with all aspects of homeschooling (choosing curriculum, record keeping, meeting the state laws, activities for the students, etc.). Even if you choose not to join a group, you can still contact one for advice.
- Choose and purchase your curriculum. What curriculum should I use? This is the hardest part. You can spend a fortune or get by on just a little. You can purchase a complete curriculum from a publisher or mix and match. You can buy your books new or used.
- Set up a record-keeping system. Most support groups provide the record-keeping forms. Your record keeping can be as simple as a daily journal or as complicated as setting up daily and weekly goals.

One homeschooling parent suggests the following: "This is what I do. I lay out my plan (the assignments for the week) in a teacher's planning book. I check them off as they are completed. Quarterly, I make a summary of what was completed and covered in each subject."

There is also online help. You can sign up for weekly newsletters to keep informed of new features and sites at www.homeschooling.about.com. Homeschooling magazines are available online or by subscription. They offer suggestions that will help you add some fun to your homeschooling day. For example: Game of the Day. Educational or just for fun, come back every day for a new game. It is a great way to reward your students for a job well done. You can even find online field trips. You can use online help to supplement your curriculum or even teach completely online. Many sites cover several subject areas (crafts, driver's education, home economics, fine arts, core subjects, and state unit studies and standards).

Getting started in homeschooling may conjure up several questions. Is homeschooling expensive? You can make the process as expensive or as inexpensive as you choose. It depends on many factors, including what kinds of materials and resources you choose to use, how many children you will be homeschooling, and whether or not you will be giving up paid employment in order to homeschool your children. Parents can easily spend a small fortune on all the wonderful learning materials and books available. On the other hand, a superior education can also be accomplished using free resources found through the public library, interlibrary loan, and learning opportunities found in your community (museums, field trips to local places of interest). If you have only one child and decide to use real-life experiences, the public library, garage sales, and thrift stores are excellent resources for materials. You may be talking about $200–$300 for the entire year. If you decide to purchase a curriculum for five children you could be looking at several thousand dollars over that same year.

How do I know which materials and resources to use? This is probably the most difficult question to answer and note that your answer may change over time. Be aware that you may make choices that will not work out. Before you think about your need, think about what learning means to you. School curriculum and methodology have evolved to reflect an environment where 25 or 30 children learn at the behest of one adult. Curriculum developed by experts for this usage has been designed for ease of teaching, but not necessarily for sparking the interest of an individual child. As a homeschooling family, you can accept as many or as few of these materials as you like. Some families like the ease and security of having a prepackaged curriculum, while others choose to make their own decisions about what is important to learn and what is useful and helpful in their daily lives. Discuss this with your children. What do they want to do? How do they learn best? Look at samples of materials before you choose. As homeschoolers, you will be in charge of your learning. Take advantage of all the adventure has to offer.

Where can I get materials and resources? These items come in all sizes and shapes. Think about building and needlework materials, cooking tools, books, magazines, motors, and gears. Other families frequent bookstores and educational supply stores. Some use rental videos. Send for catalogues that look interesting to you. Also take advantage of conferences and learning fairs to look at materials and to get ideas.

One question that plagues many homeschoolers is what if my child wants to learn something that I can't teach? Children have the most amazing ability to want to learn the one thing about which we know absolutely nothing! It is a universal attribute. Homeschooling families are blessed in having the world as their classroom. There are classes (correspondence, video, support groups, community centers, colleges, etc.) taught by experts, but many children are very capable of teaching themselves, just as adults do when they have something new they want to learn. The most powerful learning experience for a child is to have a parent learning right alongside them. Parents do not have to be experts in every area. Learn with your child or search the community for resources that will help your child learn on his or her own. When searching for "teachers" do not overlook friends, acquaintances, and business people in your community. Most people are delighted to have a young person around who is sincerely interested in what they do and know.

Many homeschoolers are concerned about the question, how will my child learn to get along in the world? This is the question homeschoolers often grimace about and call the "s" question (socialization). The real concern is whether homeschooled children will be able to function out in the world if they do not have the experiences schooled children have. Think for a moment about what schools really do. They classify and segregate children by age and ability; reinforce class, gender, and racial prejudice; and strip from children the right to any real interaction or private life. Socialization, in this respect, becomes submitting one's will to that of the group (or the person in charge). Home-educated children, because they spend so much of their time out in the real world, generally are able to communicate well with both adults and children and to have friends of all ages. They choose to spend time with others because they enjoy their company or have a similar interest, just like adults.

A few parents ask if they can work at a job and still homeschool their children. Homeschooling families have often been portrayed as "Dad going to work. Mom staying at home with the kids." The reality, for many families, is much different: single parents, working parents, and dads at home all homeschool. Grandparents homeschool grandchildren. It may take a little juggling, but it can be done.

How do I know if my children are learning? Children are always learning; they just can't help it! Just as when they were babies and toddlers, you can discover what they are learning by spending time with them and observing the growth in their understanding of the world. Parents can tell when their children are learning because they're present. You know that they can tell time when they tell you what time it is. You know they are learning to read when you spell something out to your husband and your child speaks the word. Observation as an assessment (known as "authentic assessment" and a big buzzword in education these days) acknowledges growth in understanding and skill level. Unlike standardized testing, it doesn't give a "snapshot" that attempts to quantify learning at one point in time. It is fluid and flexible and has no preconceived notions about what a child "should" be able to do. You can look at the whole person and concentrate on what your child knows, instead of what your child does not know.

What should I test my child about? Testing, like many other educational concerns, should be a personal decision. Before you make this decision, ask yourself which tests will be used and why, how might the testing process affect the learner, how will the test results be used, and are there less intrusive alternatives that can be utilized instead? Testing in the home environment, where parents are always aware of how well their children are doing, is unnecessary and intrusive. Very careful consideration should be taken before any testing is done.

Finally, homeschoolers ask about higher education. Hundreds of colleges, universities, and vocational institutions all over the nation are accepting homeschooled students. Most are thrilled with these intelligent, responsible, capable young people and many are actually recruiting them. Most of these institutions value ability and attitude over formal transcripts, diplomas, and general educational development (GED) tests. It should be noted that college is not necessarily the only or even the best route for every young person. Going to college without a clear idea of what you expect to gain can be a very expensive form of self-discovery. And for many teens that already know where they are headed, apprenticeship opportunities and other forms of "on-the-job" training can be a faster and more satisfying entry into adult life. Remember, the decision to forgo college is never irrevocable. Most institutions value older students, since they are usually enthusiastic and focused on learning.

There are a wide variety of homeschooling methods and materials available. Many homeschoolers base their work on a particular educational philosophy, such as classical education, Waldorf education, Charlotte Mason education, Gardner's Theory of Multiple Intelligences, or the Montessori method. Others use a broad combination of ideas or allow the child to develop his or her own motivation. Because homeschool laws vary widely according to state statutes, official curriculum requirements vary.

Many homeschoolers use Unit Studies and teach most subjects in the context of a central theme. For example, a unit study of American Indians would combine age-appropriate lessons in social studies (how different tribes lived), art (making Indian clothing), history (the history of the American Indian in the United States), reading (usually novels or poems by American Indian authors), science (plants grown by American Indians), and so on. The following month, the unit-study subject could change to some other broad topic of study. Homeschooling parents say that unit studies make excellent use of student time by combining several fields into one study time, and permit students to follow personal interests. Unit studies also permit children of different ages to study together. For example, in the American Indian unit, a 10th grade student might make a deerskin coat for an art project, while a first grader might make construction-paper teepees. Homeschoolers often purchase unit study guides that suggest materials, projects, and shopping lists, and supplement them with specialized curricula for math, reading, and writing.

Special materials focus on skill building. Individual subject materials usually consist of workbooks, sometimes with textbooks and a teacher's guide. Special materials are frequently used for math and primary reading. Critics say that some parents overfocus on skills while excluding social studies, science, art, and history.

All-in-one curricula are comprehensive packages covering many subjects, usually as entire year's worth. Some people call them "school in a box." They contain all the needed books and materials, including pencils and writing paper. Most such curricula were developed for isolated families who lack access to public schools, libraries, or shops. These materials typically recreate the school environment in the home and are often based on the same subject-area expectations as public schools, allowing an easy retransition into school if desired. They are among the most expensive options for homeschoolers, but are easy to use and require minimal preparation.

Always utilize community resources, educational programs at museums, community centers, athletic clubs, after-school programs, churches, science preserves, parks, and other neighborhood offerings. High school–level students often take classes at community colleges.

The majority of today's homeschoolers use an eclectic mix of materials. For instance, they might use a predesigned program for language, arts, or math, and fill in history with reading and field trips, art with classes at a community center, science through a homeschool science club, physical education with membership in local sports complexes, and so on.

One final area to mention is "unschooling." This is an area within homeschooling in which students are not directly instructed but encouraged to learn through exploring their interests. Also known as interest-led or child-led learning, unschooling attempts to provide opportunities with games and real-life problems where a child will learn without coercion. An unschooled child may choose to use texts or classroom instruction, but it is never considered central to education. Advocates for unschooling claim that children learn best by doing. A child may learn reading and math skills from playing card games, improve spelling and other writing skills because he or she is inspired to write a science-fiction story for publication, or learn local history by following a zoning or historical-status dispute.

Always research the curriculum you select. Hundreds of exhibitors lined the aisles at the last homeschooling conference I attended. There were educational games; nifty self-instructional computer math programs; complete science lab kits; history, art, and music videos; all the basics of K–12 education on CD-ROM; even some wonderful books. It all beckoned, promising to make my life easier by selling me the tools for the perfect homeschool program.

The growth of home education has created an explosion in use-at-home educational resources over the past 10 years. In addition, technological advances over the years have placed current information about all sorts of programs and resources at our fingertips. Recently surfing the World Wide Web, I read a high school homeschooler's self-devised program, downloaded a practice SAT (Scholastic Aptitude Test, a college entrance exam), and perused the "Getting started with teenagers" recommendations of a popular homeschooling program.

However, too often the plethora of information is daunting. New homeschooling families, especially those families with teenagers, feel the selections may become problematic. With the adulthood of their teens right around the corner, these parents want to do the right thing. The right thing is often defined by the statement: "I don't want to do anything that will wreck his or her chances of _____." You fill in the blank: getting into college, finding employment, joining the military, living on his or her own, and so forth. It is so easy to be scared into trading big bucks for the assurance that you are doing the right thing.

So, let's go back to the conference exhibits. After cruising the hall and eyeing the dazzling displays, I found a comfortable perch and watched the homeschooling parents intently quizzing the vendors about products, schools, and programs. I came to the conclusion that you really don't need the glitzy stuff to succeed. In fact, avoiding glitz may be the key to more productive home education.

I repeat: your community often provides better outlets for your children's exploration than any program you could buy. One parent told me that her daughter completed 4-H's Public Speaking Project two years in a row. This project required her to deliver a prepared speech, memorize and present a poem to an audience, speak extemporaneously on a topic, and compile a record of experience including an essay. This is great hands-on language arts. For this parent, membership in 4-H for her daughter was a fraction of the cost of many language arts programs; and 4-H yielded many other opportunities for education, socialization, and entertainment.

Looking first to the community for resources encourages autonomy and creative problem solving. A young homeschooler I know trades housework for pottery and Spanish lessons. Another teenage homeschooler attends her church's adult comparative religions class because she has a consuming interest in the topic and nothing is offered for her age group. A third has taught herself how to sew, using a neighbor's machine and occasional help. Yet another found algebra help through an online website.

Searching the community models learning how to learn. Children not only learn the subject, but they also learn how to locate resources to help them research any topic, an invaluable skill for adult life.

I asked several homeschooling parents the crucial question: What made you decide to homeschool? Their decision was a personal one and usually a difficult one to make.

One parent said that the continued threat of teacher's strikes, with both sides using the children as pawns made her angry. She went on to say that after the first trial year of homeschooling she loved it, loved learning with her children and spending time with them. She felt that they were allowed to excel academically in their best subjects and get one-on-one attention in the weaker areas.

Another parent said, "I'm selfish. After seeing the look on Rachel's face when she realized she had read a word on her own there was no way that I wanted someone else to enjoy those moments."

Several parents said that they simply wanted to be with their children and were convinced that they could do a better job teaching than any teacher in the school system they would attend.

One dad said that he had fun learning with his son and that academics were not about rote memorization of meaningless facts but an exploration begun out of curiosity and interest.

Another dad said that he saw his family draw closer together. Dinnertime was when discussions took place. They actually talked, discussing current events, books, and movies. They mastered new words and visited faraway places in their minds.

A grandmother said that homeschooling allows you to look for teachable moments. You can find them in the most ordinary and mundane places if you pay attention. The homeless man holding a sign that reads, "Will work for food," becomes an opportunity to discuss human rights, compassion, and welfare policy. An unusual bug crawling across the sidewalk becomes a biology lesson. Replacing a burned-out lightbulb provides an opportunity to talk about electricity. Shopping becomes a lesson in nutrition and money management, and a sudden cloudburst becomes a lesson in meteorology. Even watching television has its moments: casual sex, violence, and deep-seated human problems solved in less than an hour, provides opportunities to challenge and learn from the material being presented.

A grandfather said he works on projects with his grandkids, building birdhouses and model planes, planting a vegetable garden, and going fishing. He also tells stories about the past, turning these stories into an educational adventure.

One mom spoke in terms of revelations: One being that textbooks are the most stultifying, mind-deadening books in the world. A second revelation is that it takes about an hour and a half a day to cover everything that is covered in one day at school. Most of the school day is spent waiting for the bus ride to be over, waiting for the bell, waiting for the teacher to get organized, waiting for the teacher to handle discipline issues, and waiting in line to be marched elsewhere. It's like being put on hold. A third revelation is that the more you teach, the less they learn. You can't force knowledge on them, they have to reach out and take it. Children are born achievers. Their interest and motivation are instinctive.

A father sums it all up: "I am completely sold on homeschooling because I believe in people's desire and ability to learn wonderful things in quirky ways if they are given the opportunity."

We cannot ignore the fact that some parents are dealing with doubts. Will the eclectic approach get you where you want to go? Doubts may arise over a relaxed approach. Did you do the "right thing"? Homeschooling parents often encounter people who automatically link learning only with classroom seat time and credentialed teaching. Deal with your doubts by thinking about the students who have been homeschooled. The following conversation with a 17-year-old young lady is an example of student success. Anne displayed much more confidence than many adults. She had the nerve to insist that despite not using curriculum, not taking tests, and not studying anything in a formal manner, she was perfectly capable of learning whatever she needed to know and to do whatever she needed to do. Anne saw no sense in memorizing American history dates, reading prominent English poets, learning chemical symbols, or fighting her way through geometry proofs. When asked about the gaps in her education, she said there were none. She felt the essentials in her life were character development, the three Rs, computer literacy, everyday living skills, and being physically fit. Anne is a personable, intelligent, articulate young lady, possessing poise and confidence that many adults would envy. She obviously has a wonderful relationship with her parents, and I have no doubt Anne will achieve any goals she sets. By the way, Anne has been accepted at four major colleges based on her interview, not her American College Testing Program (ACT) scores.

If you still have doubts, there are some things you can do to reduce your anxiety about "gaps" and "not covering it all." You can:

- Immerse yourself in success stories.
- Share experiences with local, like-minded homeschooling parents.
- Review several scope and sequences (sometimes synonymous with goals, objectives, curriculum, or courses of study) from different publishers.
- Examine your definition of success. Clear your mind (of your own school experiences) and discuss often, with your children, the results you want.
- Remind yourself that teaching does not equal learning.
- Make an appointment at your local high school (if you have a teenager) and sit through an entire day of classes. Watch and listen carefully. Keep track of on-task time (reading, doing math problems, discussions, taking notes) versus administrative time (forming groups, passing out supplies, fund-raisers, attendance, correcting papers, and discipline). Observe the behavior of schooled children, and then ask yourself who should be worried about gaps.
- Focus on the donut, not the hole. List one or more positive things about each of your children. This will counteract the natural tendency that all of us have to define Johnny as a poor speller or Jenny as "no good in math."
- Motivate yourself with record keeping. If the worst-case scenario occurs and you somehow have to justify homeschooling with educational success, you will be able to do it.

- Don't take yourself too seriously. Most kids are going to turn out a certain way regardless of what we do. One child may be wired for creativity (cooking, writing, composing, drawing, acting, decorating, you name it). As a parent, you may have none of those characteristics and do nothing to encourage them. This child's creativity is independent of your efforts to "educate" him or her. Similarly, another child may have the proverbial mind-like-a-steel-trap with respect to numbers and spatial-engineering problems. Again, not a trait you have in abundance. Relax, your kid's talents will surface despite what you do.

Homeschooling produces results. Colleges and universities are recruiting homeschooled students. A homeschooler's curriculum may often include subjects not included in traditional school curriculum. Many colleges find this an advantage as they attempt to create an academically diverse student body, which in turn creates more well-rounded and self-sufficient adults.

Social development is not a concern. Most homeschoolers are active in community groups. Homeschooled children socialize with other children in the same way that schoolchildren do: outside of school, through personal friends, and through sports teams, clubs, and religious groups. Proponents agree that the social environment of traditional schools involves bullying, drug use, early sexuality, defiance, and materialism. Socialization in the wider community leads children and young adults to use adults as role models, and it prepares them for real life, encourages involvement, and helps them develop an independent understanding of themselves and their role in the world, with the freedom to reject or approve conventional values without the risk of ridicule.

In addition, I've looked teenaged homeschoolers in the eyes, talked to them, and seen thoughtful, whole, confident, compassionate, curious, kind, and joyful people who have the ability to interact with adults.

Homeschooling also results in a change in attitude. Homeschooling means dismantling the overlay of school. Stop speaking and thinking in terms of grades, semesters, school days, education, scores, tests, and performance. Replace those artificial structures and measures with ideas like morning, hungry, happy, new, learning, interesting, playing, exploring, and living.

No two homeschools are alike. The glory and strength of homeschooling is that it can embrace so many different families and so many different approaches to raising and educating children. Parents are taking responsibility for themselves. What happens when we take responsibility for families? Amazing things! We discover that children learn and do better outside of school. We take control of our time and spend it on what is most important to us. We set our own schedules and timetables for learning, going to a park on a beautiful day, reading stories late at night, or sleeping as much as we need. We take control of space as we arrange our homes in ways that are comfortable for us, learn from the whole world, enjoy direct experience, and so much more.

Homeschooling results in stronger families by giving them time together, time to get to know each other, to work and play, to laugh and cry, and to make mistakes and then correct them. Parents have a chance to raise their children in the way they want them raised. Siblings learn to live closely with each other, to appreciate each other's strengths, to accept weaknesses, and to be there for each other.

Parents are learning with their children and from their children they learn to use common sense, to observe the world, learn what they need to know, and to stop worrying about what someone else thinks.

It is estimated that 600,000 to over 1 million children in the United States are educated at home. Parents choose to do so because they want to teach values. They want less structured learning than typical public or private schools provide, and many parents want greater control over the material their child learns.

Some parents organize homeschools like conventional schools, with structured, daily activities. Others view all of life as an opportunity for learning and use a flexible schedule. Most provide educational opportunity outside as well as inside the home. Children may visit a museum, work in a garden, or serve an apprenticeship. Some parents use textbooks; others create their own materials.

Critics say that homeschooled children may not have enough social contact with other children, especially those from different backgrounds or cultures. Critics also say that the average parent is not qualified to teach. The truth is that most homeschooled children achieve academic scores equal to or better than public school students on college entrance exams, achievement tests, and social development tests.

Parents relate that, first and foremost, homeschools are distinctive and that we must appreciate and celebrate that fact. The most important part of homeschooling includes taking responsibility for our families, strengthening our families, and growing with our children. If we take our homeschooling freedoms for granted, we are very likely to lose them. But if we work to understand and maintain the distinctiveness of homeschooling, we will strengthen our freedoms.

Crossing the threshold of the 21st century, family freedom in education is capturing imaginations by the hundreds of thousands. This is homeschooling, and it has been around long enough to stir up society's notions about the way we go about educating our children.

Imagine for a moment that your family starts off every morning with that Friday afternoon feeling of freedom. Imagine that instead of being dictated by a schedule imposed on your family by others, learning now weaves smoothly from one day to the next, seamlessly joining the rhythm of family life. Imagine learning becoming an extended excursion into a great wide world of knowledge with stops at points of interest along the way.

Homeschooling is a journey that is accomplished from the comfort, warmth, and security of home, guided by your child's first and most important teacher, you.

Homeschooling is not just an exciting idea of freedom in education; it's a successful one, too. In 2005, the Riverside Publishing Company released the Iowa Basic Achievement Test scores of 16,000 home-educated students. The test is one of several standardized tests commonly administered in schools. Children taught at home averaged in the 87 percentile, 37 percent above what the testing company deems average ability.

At the most basic level, homeschooling is your family taking full responsibility for the education of your own children. Accepting this responsibility takes your family off the public school learning path. It frees your child from a one-size-fits-all curriculum, from mandatory programs having less to do with academics and much more to do with attitude adjustment, from a high student-to-teacher ratio, and from negative peer pressure and influence. It also frees your family from the less obvious: a time schedule ill-suited to your family's needs, the high cost of the latest fashion trends, and a lack of time for exposure to normal socialization available in the larger community.

Once off the public school learning path, your family creates its own educational path, going wherever you want to go. One family starts at 8 a.m. right after breakfast, another at 9:30 a.m. after a leisurely breakfast and completing household chores. One does science experiments in the kitchen; another joins with fellow homeschoolers at the home of a support group member. One ends the day by going to the playground; another volunteers at the humane society. One family sticks to the curriculum provider's timetable; another follows along for three months and then tosses the whole thing in the trash.

The very nature of the freedom inherent in accepting educational responsibility through homeschooling creates an infinite variety of ways your family may go about its learning day. Homeschoolers blaze unexplored trails every day. It depends on who you ask.

Homeschooling parents relate that in their own homeschools, they can strongly emphasize the home part of homeschooling and the ways in which homeschooling allows them to take responsibility for themselves and strengthens their families. They can keep their focus on what they have decided is most important. They can decide not to evaluate their homeschools using conventional school standards (test scores, curriculum directions, credits acquired). They can share with educators their ideas on how homeschooling is distinctive and how it strengthens their families. They can also share their conviction and experiences that homeschooling works.

Homeschoolers are growing into mature, responsible adults who are making important contributions to our society, regardless of their approach to academics. Through homeschooling, our children are finding the space they need to develop confidence, to discover their passions, to identify the unique contributions they have to make to the world, and to dare to soar.

7

PRIVATE SCHOOLS: AN INVESTMENT IN THE FUTURE

> There is always one unexpected little moment in life when a door opens and lets the future in.
>
> —Graham Greene

"What better investment can you make in your child's future?" That's how Steve Franklin explains why he is paying for his son to attend a private school in Richmond, Virginia. He goes on to say that the advantages of private education include daily tutorials, individual teacher conferences several times a year, and such small classes his son "can't hide in the back of the room" (Costen, 2005).

That is also why the 72 private schools in the Richmond area are being attended by some 16,700 kindergarteners to high school seniors. The Council for American Private Education reports there are more than 27,000 private schools in the United States, with an enrollment of more than 6 million students.

Smaller classes, more individualized attention, well-behaved student bodies, and better preparation for college are some advantages to which private school administrators attribute this constant growth. The growth in turn enables the schools to admit students most likely to benefit from their particular programs and personality.

Everyone has to apply for admission. Many schools also give admission tests (even to would-be first graders) in order to make sure the student will benefit from their curriculum.

Richmond private schools, as many private schools nationwide, have a wide range of grade levels, subjects, and sponsorships by churches.

Each school has its own personality. For example, some offer more foreign languages while others favor special art or music classes. One includes computer skills at early grade levels; others concentrate on religion or classical studies, and many favor athletics.

Whatever the extras may be, each private school stresses academic excellence and measures success by preparing every student to have the opportunity to go on to higher education. The private high schools in Richmond report about 95% to 100% college admission with a large number of seniors getting early acceptance.

Parents like Steve Franklin are willing to spend the money on their children's education now. The following schools are examples of Richmond's best.

Benedictine is a Catholic boy's military high school (enrollment 276, tuition $10,600) that features junior reserve officers' training corps (JROTC), 4 years of theology, an award-winning arts program and robotics, as well as a 4-year leadership awareness series. Advantages cited are Christian values, small classes, individual attention, and academic opportunities. Parent August Wallmeyer says that 97% of the last graduating class went on to college, and the students feel a sense of community.

Collegiate has 1,526 K–12 students (tuition $14,000) with an emphasis on academic and character development. Advantages include an arts center, science buildings with 10 labs, two libraries, eight athletic fields, and eight tennis courts. Parent Mrs. Palmer Garson says that personal focus on the individual is the prime advantage of private schools.

Raymond Christian School is a coeducational K–12 Baptist school with 480 students (tuition $4,500). Emphasis is on character, values, and biblical principles. Every high school student is required to do documented community service. Parent Randy Ray, whose three children attend the school, says that all are achieving beyond grade level and are being taught moral values.

St. Gertrude is a Catholic girls high school attended by 265 students (tuition $9,100). The students are required to do community service at

Meals on Wheels or Freedom House, as part of the 4-year theology program. The school stresses an atmosphere conducive to learning where a student can grow not only academically and physically, but also emotionally and spiritually. Parent Anna Johnson says that the faculty is molding who our daughters will be for the rest of their lives.

Finally, Steward School's enrollment is 578 for grades K–12 with tuition from $12,500 to $14,000. Its 37-acre location includes five academic buildings, an athletic center, three athletic fields, and six tennis courts. Emphasis is on a strong academic program with photography, sculpture, computer graphics, and dance. Parent Mrs. Timothy Carter says that her three children are not getting just a "cookie-cutter education. They are getting individualized and nurturing attention. It's not just about grades, it's about developing character and fortitude."

Private education in the United States is defined as programs of instruction that are created, controlled, operated, and principally financed by private individuals and groups rather than by the government. Private schools are not administered by local or national government and retain the right to select their student body. These schools are funded in whole or in part by charging their students tuition rather than using public funds. The amount of tuition varies widely according to the type of school and the level of education offered. Although the cost of private education is beyond the reach of many American families, most private schools offer some form of financial aid to low-income applicants. In addition to revenue generated by tuition payments, private schools are supported mainly by funds from other private sources, such as religious organizations, endowments, grants, and charitable donations.

More than 6 million students (11.5% of the nation's elementary and secondary school population) are attending private schools according to a report released by the U.S. Department of Education's National Center for Education statistics in 2005. In addition, the report says that 24% of all elementary and secondary schools in the United States are private.

What types of private schools exist in the United States? Private schools may be broadly classified as either religious or nonsectarian (nonreligious) institutions. Various branches of the Catholic Church support the most common types of religious schools in the United States. Religiously affiliated schools (also called parochial schools) form a distinct category of private school. Such schools teach religious lessons, often alongside a secular education, to instill religious knowledge and a strong religious identity in the students who attend.

Another category of private school is the preparatory school or "prep school." These are secondary schools that are designed to prepare a student for higher education. Many of these schools are highly selective, accepting only a very small percentage of applicants. Tuition at prep schools varies from school to school. High tuition, schools claim, is used to pay higher salaries for the best teachers and is also used to provide enriched learning environments and services such as libraries, science labs, and computers. Graduates of prep schools are often actively sought by colleges due to the colleges' confidence that the students will be well educated.

Many private schools are boarding schools and offer lodging to students in addition to academic instruction. Some military schools fall in this category and are privately owned and operated as well.

Some trade or vocational schools are also private schools where students can learn skills in a trade, which they intend to make their future occupation. A variety of trade schools exist from cosmetology schools to prestigious schools for the performing arts.

Finally, special assistance schools aim to improve the lives of their students by providing services tailored to very specific needs of individual students. Such schools include tutoring schools and schools to assist the learning of handicapped children.

Both religious and nonsectarian private schools may feature other distinguishing characteristics such as single-sex enrollment or residential facilities.

The term *independent school* refers to any private school that is independently governed by a board of trustees, rather than by a church or religious organization. Independent schools may have a religious or nonsectarian orientation. They are financed primarily by tuition, fees, charitable contributions, and income from investments, rather than by taxes or church funds.

RELIGIOUS SCHOOLS

Approximately 85% of all private school students attend schools affiliated with religious organizations, and about 50% of all private school students attend Catholic schools. However, private religious schools in the United States encompass a remarkable diversity of religious affiliations, educational objectives, and curriculums. Some religiously affiliated schools operate under the principle that religious instruction should be a key element in the daily education of children. Others attempt to provide some religious content but emphasize traditional academics. Many private religious schools strive to offer an alternative to the relatively secular (nonreligious) spirit of public schools.

Another name for religious schools is parochial schools, a type of private school, which engages in religious instruction in addition to conventional education. Parochial schools are typically grammar schools or high schools run by churches or parishes. In the United States such schools are maintained by a number of religious groups including Lutherans, Seventh-Day Adventists, Orthodox Jews, Muslims, and evangelical Protestant churches. However, the most numerous are those attached to the Roman Catholic parishes.

Catholic Schools

The Catholic parochial school system developed in the 19th century as a response to what was seen as Protestant domination of the public school system in America. For example, many public schools required students to read the King James Version of the Bible, the version authorized by Protestant churches but not by the Catholic Church. A group of American bishops met in the Third Plenary Council of Baltimore (1884) to plan for the establishment of a comprehensive parochial school system. Local churches were directed to establish elementary schools for the education of the parish children. In time, a number of secondary schools supported by a diocese and encompassing a number of parish schools were also established. Both the elementary and secondary schools developed a religious curriculum emphasizing Catholic doctrine along with a secular curriculum very similar to that of the public schools.

In the middle of the 20th century, much of Catholic parochial education's structure began to change. The ecumenical spirit generated by the Second Vatican Council (1962–1965) convinced many Roman Catholics that the religious education of the parochial school was too separatist.

Moreover, parochial schools suffered from the criticism that public schools provided a better secular education at less cost. Because of such criticisms, Catholic schools were forced to hire lay teachers, who came to account for an increasingly larger proportion of the faculty. Beginning in the mid-1960s, Roman Catholic schools began to encounter severe financial problems, many parish schools were closed, and the Catholic school population dropped sharply.

Because of the public concern for education today, Catholic schools are once again on the rise. Catholic schools today develop their students through participation in the sacramental life of the church, study in religion and theology, a full curriculum in secular subjects, and a variety of extracurricular activities. In the United States, Catholic schools are accredited by independent and/or state agencies, and all teachers are certified. Catholic elementary and secondary schools receive virtually no government funding and are supported through tuition payments and fund-raising. Tuition at Catholic parochial and diocesan schools is generally low compared to other private schools because parishes and dioceses subsidize part of the school expenses. In addition parents of Catholic parochial students can apply for tax subsidies or credits. Under the "child-benefit theory," government aid is provided to the students in Catholic schools, rather than to the schools themselves.

Religion is included in the learning experience and at some schools uniforms are required for students.

A few Catholic schools are controlled by independent religious orders of the Catholic Church, such as Jesuits, Benedictines, and Christian Brothers. These schools usually offer only high school level instruction, and their academic programs are typically more demanding than either parochial or diocesan schools.

Catholic schools today are showing successful programs and increasing enrollments. Many inner-city Catholic schools with limited budgets are frequently producing better academic results than heavily funded public schools.

At Loyola Catholic School in Denver, Colorado's inner city, more than 80% of the students are African American, and more than half of the students are non-Catholic. Many struggle with poverty. But like its Catholic sister schools elsewhere in the inner city, Loyola has created a superior learning environment with active parental support. It boasts an atmosphere of positive discipline, strong moral foundations, and a competitive academic program. As a result, Loyola students learn not merely facts, but the mutual respect and personal pride that come from genuine achievement. Dropout rates are low, graduation rates are high, and the bureaucracies are small. Loyola accomplishes all this at a cost of $2,500 per student versus $5,000 per student in the Denver public schools.

Catholic schools like Loyola are doing an outstanding job of serving low-income and culturally diverse students, and they are eager to do more.

Other Religious Schools

Non-Catholic, religiously oriented schools enroll 34% of all private school students in the United States. Most of these are supported by various Protestant organizations. The majority of Protestant schools are affiliated with the so-called conservative Christian associations. Many are operated by individual churches like Christ the King Lutheran in St. Paul, Minnesota, or John the Baptist [Baptist] School in Memphis, Tennessee. Since the 1960s the number of conservative Christian schools and their enrollments has grown more rapidly than any other type of private school.

One other type of religious private school is called the Christian school, which is a school run on Christian principles or by a Christian organization. The nature of Christian schools varies enormously from county to county according to the religious and educational culture of the region.

In the United States religion is generally not taught by the state-funded educational system, under the principle of separation of church and state. Christian schools are therefore privately run. Parents who want their children taught according to Christian principles can choose to send their children to such schools, but unless the school is subsidized by their church, or is part of a school choice or education voucher program funded by the government, they must pay tuition. Some Christian schools are large and well funded, while others are small and rely on volunteers from the community.

One emerging movement among Christian schools is the return to the traditional subjects and form of education known as classical education. Grand Haven Christian School, founded in 1880 in Grand Haven, Michigan, is considered one of the top Christian schools in the nation. Parents created a school that actively integrated their Christian faith into the whole curriculum.

Non-Christian religious organizations have also established many private schools, particularly during the second half of the 20th century. Among the most common are Jewish schools, often called Hebrew day schools.

There are several advantages to having a parochial school education. Parents relate that some of the advantages their sons and daughters receive at a parochial school (whether Catholic, Lutheran, Baptist, etc.) are a curriculum that focuses on teaching basic skills and an atmosphere that demands respect for authority and self-discipline. Plus, considerable attention is usually focused on maintaining order. There are fewer discipline issues because parochial schools can be selective about whom they admit and are under no obligation to retain children who do not follow the rules. The students also have the opportunity to be with peers who have similar values and to be part of a faith community.

Parents also stress that prospective parochial school parents should compare their choice of parochial school with a public school. Look at the curricula and decide which one best fits/meets your child's needs. Compare copyright dates on textbooks. While old math and English textbooks can be good instructional tools, old history and geography books will not give your child a solid knowledge of recent events and boundary changes. Consider also such things as class size, achievement test scores, the teaching staff, and the emphasis on order and discipline.

NONSECTARIAN PRIVATE SCHOOLS

Nonsectarian, or secular, private schools are usually not affiliated with any religion or church. These schools generally emphasize the development of moral character more than the study of organized religion. Other independent schools may have highly specialized educational programs that focus on particular subjects, such as science, math, or the performing arts.

Independent college preparatory schools (prep schools) are generally the wealthiest, best known, and most expensive of all private schools. Some of the most prestigious preparatory boarding schools, such as Phillips Academy in Andover, Massachusetts, and Phillips Exeter Academy in Exeter, New Hampshire, draw students from across the nation and, increasingly, from around the world. Some of the most prestigious preparatory day schools include the Dalton School and the Brearley School in New York City; Roxbury Latin School in Boston, Massachusetts; Francis W. Parker School in Chicago, Illinois; and Lakeside School in Seattle, Washington.

Other examples of nonsectarian private schools include military academies, boarding schools, and Montessori schools. These schools will be described in more detail in the following paragraphs.

Preparatory Schools

In the United States, a preparatory school or prep school is usually a private high school designed to prepare a student for higher education. Many are boarding schools; often, such schools are highly selective and academically challenging and are largely independent of state or local control. Prep schools are very expensive, with the high tuition used to pay excellent teachers and provide enriched learning environments, through features such as large libraries, advanced science laboratories, and new computers. New England prep schools, in particular, place a strong emphasis on sports.

College prep schools often place an emphasis on offering a wide variety of advanced placement courses, rigorous academic programs, and small class sizes of 20 students or less. Admission is rigorously selective and often based on standardized college entrance exams like the Scholastic Aptitude Test (SAT).

Many colleges and universities actively recruit prep school students because the students have been prepared for higher education, usually achieving higher-than-average SAT scores.

Because these schools pay very well (and/or offer superior working conditions), preparatory schools are often able to recruit faculty and staff with graduate degrees from the top universities, particularly the Ivy League schools. In contrast, many teachers at public schools usually hold only a bachelor's degree (which may or may not even be in the field that they teach) and a teaching certificate.

Some of the American preparatory schools worth noting are: Atlanta International School (Atlanta, Georgia), Avon Old Farms School (Avon, Connecticut), the Buckley School (Los Angeles, California), Fordham Preparatory School (Washington, D.C.), Lawrence Academy at Groton (Groton, Massachusetts), Middlesex School (Concord, Massachusetts), Pembroke Hill School (Kansas City, Missouri), St. Ignatius College Prep (Chicago, Illinois), and St. Paul Academy and Summit School (St. Paul, Minnesota).

Lawrence Academy is a coeducational preparatory school located in Groton, Massachusetts. It was founded by Samuel Lawrence in 1793 as Groton Academy and chartered by Governor John Hancock. The school changed its name in 1845 to honor Amos, Abbott, and William Lawrence, famed alumni, and major benefactors during that era.

Lawrence Academy has gained renown for excellent university preparation and an innovative curriculum, engendering experiential learning. Signature programs include Winterim, a 2-week adventure term, and Independent Immersion, a year-long program in which a student focuses on a single endeavor, as though at a conservatory. Lawrence Academy aims to stimulate creative thinking and foster active participation in society.

Lawrence Academy is seated upon 100 acres of rolling countryside 31 miles northwest of Boston. Architecturally, its campus features a mixture of historic, Federalist-era houses and neo-Georgian academic buildings. Each year Lawrence Academy enrolls approximately 375 students (200 are boarding students) through admission that is highly selective. The student-teacher ratio is seven to one, with an average class size of 11 students. Tuition is approximately $34,000 for boarders and $26,400 for day students. Thirty percent of the students receive financial aid to attend.

The academy is close to several urban centers so that students can take advantage of urban social, cultural, and recreational offerings, yet is far enough removed so that students can enjoy the quiet, peaceful character of the New England countryside. The school is accredited by the New England Association of Schools and Colleges and is a member of the New England Preparatory School Athletic Council. One hundred percent of graduates go on to college.

Military Schools and Military Academies

In the United States the term *military school* primarily refers to precollegiate (middle and high school) institutions. The term *military academy* commonly refers to all precollegiate, collegiate, and postcollegiate institutions.

A military school teaches various ages (middle school, high school, or both) in a manner that includes military traditions and training in military subjects. Many military schools are also boarding schools and are usually privately run institutions.

A common misperception often results because some states have chosen to house their child criminal populations in high-security boarding schools that are run in a manner similar to military boarding schools. These state-operated schools attempt to emulate the high standards of established military boarding schools in the hope that a strict structural environment can reform these children. This may or may not be true. However, this should not reflect on the long and distinguished history of military schools; they are traditionally associated with high academic achievement, solid college preparatory curriculums, schooling in the military arts, and considerably esteemed graduates.

Two renowned military academies come to mind. Valley Forge Military Academy is an all-male middle school and high school located in Wayne, Pennsylvania. General Milton Baker founded the school in 1928. New cadets come in as plebes and have 6 weeks of intense training and a test in order to earn their cap-shield, which gives cadets certain privileges (phone use, computer time, etc). The main purpose of the middle school and high school is to educate young men, within a disciplined academic and military environment, so they are fully prepared to meet their responsibilities as citizen leaders in a manner that reflects alertness in mind, soundness in body, consideration of others, and a high sense of duty, honor, loyalty, and courage. This prepares students for West Point and other military academies. Famed cadets who attended Valley Forge include General Norman Schwarzkopf and J. D. Salinger.

Oak Ridge Military Academy is a coeducational school that was established in 1852 in Oak Ridge, North Carolina. It offers, within a military structure, a college-preparatory curriculum that develops well-rounded young men and women who are equipped to succeed in college and have the self-discipline, integrity, and leadership skills necessary to reach their potential in life.

Boarding Schools

A boarding school is a self-contained educational institution where students not only study but also live. Boarding schools provide housing and academic instruction to students at the same place.

The term *boarding school* refers to classic British boarding schools, and most boarding schools in the United States and even around the world are modeled on this classic British institution. These schools have specified rooms or allotted areas for different activities that occur throughout the day as defined by the boarding school administrators. These activities have a predefined structure and time set by the institution. The predefined schedules and norms are to be strictly followed, the failure of which could earn punishment. These rooms include the dormitory where students share sleeping quarters, the dining area where meals are served on fixed schedules, and the study hall where students do their academic work. Most boarding schools have grounds for play and athletics and other activities.

Students may be sent to boarding schools between the ages of 2 (Alaska only) and 18. Children can be sent to any number of specific types of boarding schools, from nursery boarding schools (or kindergarten boarding schools) to senior preparatory boarding schools. The amount of time a child spends in boarding school also varies considerably, from a brief period of one year to more than 12 years.

As stated earlier, boarding schools are a form of residential school systems; however, not all residential schools are "classic" boarding schools. Some boarding schools include residential schools for disabled students (for students who are blind), special needs schools (for mentally challenged students), and reservation schools where some children stay at the school but also have everyday contact with their parents during specified hours.

College prep boarding schools are the most common. There are also all-boys or all-girls boarding schools and preprofessional arts schools, training students in music, visual arts, theater, ballet, and creative writing. There are religious boarding schools, emphasizing a particular religion or spiritual growth program.

Why would you choose a boarding school for your child? Sending a child to boarding school isn't an easy decision. He or she will need to adjust to a new environment. The physical separation from family and friends can make the move emotionally difficult. Financial costs are also a consideration. Is it worth it? Couldn't a private day program offer the same education and experience?

Parents who choose boarding school for their children have cited the following reasons for sending them:

- Attention to students. Boarding schools generally have small class sizes, which help teachers engage every student in the classroom.
- Quality of the faculty. The majority of boarding school faculty has advanced degrees in either education or another specialty.
- Quality of resources. Student resources at boarding schools (library, theater facilities, laboratories, or athletic complexes) are often superior to local options.
- Challenging academics. High standards are the focus and students are pushed to ask "why," become inquisitive, and tackle challenging problems.
- Broad and diverse offerings. Course selections at boarding schools tend to be quite diverse, offer plenty of advanced placement options, and offer a wide variety of topics. Athletics and extracurricular options tend to be broad as well, which encourages students to try new things. Many boarding schools also offer opportunities to study in different countries for a term.
- College counseling. The counseling departments at boarding schools are well staffed and taken quite seriously. Counselors are experienced in helping applicants identify appropriate schools and advising them on getting into competitive institutions.

Boarding school alumni say that they really liked making choices that matter and taking responsibility for themselves. Boarding school students have plenty of support from faculty, advisors, and peers, but will learn to take care of themselves and take responsibility for their own actions to a much greater degree than if they were living at home. While there is definitely structure within the boarding school day, students still need to make choices about how to spend their time, what activities and opportunities to take, and how to create a reasonable balance between work and play. Students will be able to make choices that have a direct impact on the things they learn and the life they lead at the school.

Some say that it is important for children to be in an environment where trying new things is encouraged. Sending your child to boarding school means taking a risk because you think the reward will be worthwhile. Boarding school students will repeatedly make ventures into the unknown where they will meet new people, find their place in a new community, learn new skills and subjects, and challenge themselves to a higher academic standard. They will experience personal growth, increase confidence, and get excellent preparation for college.

Others say that students can have a lot of fun and will form intense friendships. Living at boarding school is like living in a house with a bunch of your closest friends. Dorm mates often become the closest of friends and provide a support network for each other. Boarding schools actively aim to recruit students from a wide range of geographic, racial, and socioeconomic backgrounds, so your child will be exposed to a wide range of individuals and cultures. Students are also exposed to faculty in a multitude of settings throughout the day; for example, the classroom (as teachers), athletic fields (as coaches), extracurricular groups (as advisers), and dorm settings (as dorm supervisors). Since the faculty is easily accessible throughout the day, getting academic help is usually a lot easier. Learning and mentorship opportunities abound.

Finally, your child will be a part of a proud community. The traditions and history behind many boarding schools drive the character of each school, and influence each student who goes there.

One alumnus went on to say that education takes on a broad meaning at boarding schools. The schools recognize that they often have an explicit mission to not only educate students in the classroom, but to also help them become better rounded individuals.

Even if you are just starting your boarding school research, there is a good chance you already have an impression of what boarding school is like. This impression might come from books you've read, such as *The Catcher in the Rye* or *A Separate Peace*. It also might have come from movies you have watched like *Dead Poet's Society* or *School Ties*.

These stories, while entertaining, take place in boarding school settings that are different from what you will find today. If Holden Caulfield were to return to school for Alumni Day 2007, he would find that the world of proctors and prefects, dorm teas, and Mr. Chips has undergone a millennial thaw. Most of the students attending boarding schools packed their bags willingly and are in daily e-mail contact with Mom and Dad. The ivy is no longer one shade of green. Students are as likely to room with a real prince of Thailand as with the Fresh Prince of Bel Air, as schools reach further into the public high schools for the majority of their students, making admissions more competitive than ever. The monastic life of formal dinners, daily chapel, and cold showers has given way to internationally themed meals, contemporary ecumenism, and interdorm dances.

The perception of boarding school is changing but there are still some lingering myths that can make you mistakenly think that your child would not fit in. Beware of the following:

- Myth. You must be very wealthy to attend a boarding school. Today, approximately one-third of all boarding school students receive financial aid in the form of grants, loans, or merit awards/scholarships.
- Myth. Diversity is rare at boarding schools. More than a quarter of all boarding school students are children of color.
- Myth. Kids don't have fun at boarding school. Curfews and rules will be part of the life at any boarding school but it also is an environment that is conducive to making incredible friends and having fun in the process. Keep in mind that while strong academics are a key focus for boarding schools, they also strive to foster independence in students, giving them choices in how they spend their time and what activities to choose. This process of growth in independence, meeting new people, and pursuing their interests is often fun and very rewarding.
- Myth. Boarding school is for kids who are having trouble at home. Students are eager to attend; they are not being forced to attend for disciplinary reasons.
- Myth. It will be hard for the student to keep in touch with family. Boarding school students and their families are fortunate that it is easier than ever to stay connected. The Internet is redefining com-

munication. Boarding schools offer Internet access for their students, with most having access in each building and many in each bedroom. Cell phones can also be helpful in keeping families connected.
- Keep an open mind about what you think boarding school might be like. The best way to learn is to visit a school. You can learn the most by simply being on campus and talking to current students about their experiences.

Let's visit some boarding schools that are examples of current interest to many parents and students. Avon Old Farms is an all-boys boarding school located in Avon, Connecticut. Theodate Pope Riddle, a *Lusitania* survivor and master architect, founded it. The school opened in 1927 and draws its students from all over the country. It is best known for its athletic program, especially hockey. Miss Porter's School is a prep boarding school for girls located in Farmington, Connecticut. Sarah Porter founded it in 1843, with an eye to educating the elite young women of the eastern seaboard. Girls who graduate continue their education by attending prestigious universities such as Harvard and Yale. Jacqueline Kennedy Onassis is the most renowned alumnus from this school. St. Andrew's School is a coeducational boarding school serving grades 9–12 and is located in Middletown, Delaware. It was founded in 1929 as a small Episcopalian prep school. The school has an endowment of about $170 million, making it the second richest school per capita in the country. While the school has become more secular in nature, it still retains much of its Episcopal tradition. The campus remains largely free of drugs and other common teen problems. Academically, St. Andrews is one of the finest schools in the nation and is world famous for its English Department.

Also worth mentioning is the Academy, a private boarding school for adolescents 12 to 18 years of age who are struggling in their school, home, or community. Common characteristics of students who enter the Academy may include low scholastic performance despite high potential, anger and defiance toward authority, moderate drug abuse, decreased self-esteem, and poor behavior, which is damaging their chances for a positive future. Located in Coral Island, Oregon, the school's purpose is "awakening values through commitment and achievement." The staff believes that teens that take committed action to create great lives through personal and academic achievement create greatness for themselves and within their relationships. The staff also believes that all teens possess these capabilities if they are awakened through emotional inspiration and academic challenge.

Montessori Schools

The education of the child is of profound importance to anyone dedicated to achieving "the best within us." What are the child's nature and needs? How are they different from those of an adult? How can we best foster the child's development so as to help him maximize his potential for productivity and happiness in life? It appears that the philosophy of the child developed by Italian physician and teacher Maria Montessori is most consistent with many educators' views of human nature, needs, and values.

Maria Montessori, the first woman to graduate from the University of Rome Medical School, became a doctor in 1896. Her first post was in the university's psychiatric clinic.

In that day and age, mentally handicapped children were considered a medical problem rather than an educational one, and were often kept in hospitals for the insane. Montessori's visits with children in Roman insane asylums prompted her to study the works of Itard (1775–1838) and Seguin (1812–1880), two French-born pioneers in education for the mentally deficient.

In 1899, Montessori became director of the State Orthophrenic School, where her work with the mentally handicapped was so successful that the majority of her students were able to pass the state education exams. While other educators exclaimed over this phenomenal success, Montessori pondered its implication for normal children. If the mentally handicapped could do as well on the exams as normal children, in what poor state must these normal children be. This reflection led her to devote her life to education.

Montessori opened her first Casa dei Bambini (Children's House) in 1907. It served 4- to 7-year-olds from low-income families in a full-day program. She applied the methods and materials she had developed for the mentally handicapped to children of normal intelligence. Montessori also spent a great deal of time observing and meditating on what children did with her materials, what brought out their best learning and their greatest enthusiasm.

As a result of Montessori's achievements, her method spread rapidly throughout Europe and the Far East. Schools grew in number in Europe and India, and by 1915 over 100 Montessori schools had opened in America. However, after 1920, Montessori methods were all but forgotten in the United States until the late 1950s. Then a second Montessori movement began with a set of private schools serving an almost entirely middle-class population. By the late 1960s, parents in several school districts began to agitate for public schools to offer the Montessori model for their elementary school children who had graduated from private Montessori preschools. This push was given a boost by the availability of federal funds for magnet programs. In the United States today, there are over 5,000 private Montessori schools and more than 200 public Montessori schools.

Montessori education is a child-centered and developmentally focused approach that has proven effective for children across cultural divisions and socioeconomic levels. There continues to be a growing interest in this educational approach as a way to meet the diverse needs of individual students while preparing all students for the challenges of life in an increasingly global society.

According to Maria Montessori, "a child's work is to create the person she/he will become" (Lilliard, 1972, p. 5). To carry out this self-construction, children have innate mental powers, but they must be free to use these powers. For this reason, a Montessori classroom provides freedom while maintaining an environment that encourages a sense of order and self-discipline.

Montessori recognized that the senses must be educated first in the development of the intellect. Consequently, she created a vast array of special learning materials. These materials are self-correcting, that is, from their use, the child discovers for himself whether he or she has the right answer. This feature of her materials encourages the child to be concerned with facts and truth, rather than with what adults say is right and wrong.

Montessori classes are made up of children in a 3-year age range. Preschools have 3- and 4-year-olds and kindergarteners, elementary classes have first, second, and third graders, and so on.

Montessori materials are designed for use by individual students or small groups, rather than as teacher presentation aids. In math, materials represent math concepts, such as fractions and decimals. In geography, students work with puzzle maps, in which each continent has been made into a puzzle, the pieces of which are countries.

The most important criterion for an elementary Montessori class is student activity. For 3–4 hours a day, students engage in individual and small group work of their choice. The teacher guides these choices. Another important aspect of Montessori classes is an attitude of cooperation rather than competition. It is common for students to ask their peers for help. In keeping with a reduced emphasis on conventional testing, answers to problems are made available to students. Although public Montessori schools comply with the requirements for achievement tests, many Montessorians see these tests as being irrelevant to much of what students learn.

Finally, the development of individual responsibility is emphasized. The children maintain the classroom and materials, and participate in developing class rules. Respect for people and the property and ideas of others are primary values in a Montessori classroom.

The Montessori method always places its principles and activities in the broad context of the importance of human life and development, intelligence, and free will. One of the cornerstones is the presentation of knowledge as an integrated whole, emphasizing conceptual relationships between different branches of learning and the placement of knowledge in its historical context.

Montessori is a popular alternative to traditional public school education and is successful in terms of achievement. Many successful magnet programs in the public schools have been able to integrate state requirements and Montessori requirements. By and large, Montessori programs are successful magnets in attracting and educating students.

CHARACTERISTICS OF PRIVATE SCHOOLS

Unlike public schools, which are controlled by state and local governments, private schools in the United States are relatively free from governmental regulation. Consequently, private schools vary considerably in their philosophy, mission, and educational methods. Nevertheless, private schools typically share certain characteristics that distinguish them from public schools. These include a decentralized system of governance, higher expectations, small enrollment and class size, and shared values.

When looking at decentralized governance, we note that most private schools are governed by some larger entity, such as local church or Catholic diocese. Their own boards of directors or trustees generally govern private secular schools. Private schools generally seek periodic review, or accreditation, by an independent agency to maintain their reputation and to qualify for certain governmental assistance.

Regardless of their organizational structure, private schools are largely free to manage their own affairs. They can choose their students, their faculty, and their curriculum; and make their own internal rules. In some cases, private schools are not wholly free from government regulation. State constitutions permit states to regulate all schools, both public and private, to a reasonable degree. For example, a state might require all schools to teach a particular subject, such as the state's history. Most states require private schools to obtain a state charter that recognizes their status as a private, nonprofit corporation. Such incorporation enables a school to seek exemption from paying taxes and increases tax incentives for individuals to make charitable gifts to a school. Private schools are also subject to numerous state and federal regulations concerning the health and safety of students and staff. Nonprofit private schools must also abide by federal laws protecting against discrimination.

The internal governance of most private schools differs from that of most public schools in several respects. In private schools, authority is concentrated in the individual schools rather than in the administrative offices of school districts. In addition, private school principals often have considerably more authority than their counterparts in public schools. This is usually true even for Catholic diocesan schools. Teachers in private schools also tend to have more authority over curriculum decisions than do public school teachers. In private schools run by a board of trustees, parents of current and former students often constitute a board majority.

Higher academic expectations are the focus of most private schools. Most private schools have relatively high expectations for academic achievement. For example, unlike all but a few public schools, more than 20% of all private elementary schools and more than 30% of private secondary schools require applicants to pass some kind of academic test before being granted admittance. On measures of academic expectations, such as the amount and difficulty of homework assigned, private schools generally demand more of their students than do public schools. Private schools are also more likely than public schools to focus on preparing for college. Unlike most public high schools, few private high schools offer vocational, technical, commercial, or other programs targeted to students who will not pursue a college education. As a result, private high school students are much more likely to apply to college than are public school students.

The National Center for Educational Statistics (NCES), in its 2005 report to Congress on the condition of education highlights the following:

- Private school students are more likely than public school students to complete a teacher's or advanced degree by their mid-twenties.
- Private school students generally perform higher than their public school counterparts on standardized achievement tests.
- Private school students typically have more demanding graduation requirements than do public high schools.
- Private school graduates are more likely than their peers in public schools to have completed advanced level courses in English, math, and science.
- Private high schools are four times more likely than public high schools to have a community service requirement for graduation.
- Private school teachers are more likely to report having a positive influence on teaching practices, academic standards, and school policies.

Private schools are typically much smaller than public schools. Eighty percent of all private schools have enrollments under 300. Although large public schools often offer a wider range of academic programs and support services, many parents think that smaller schools are easier to manage and create a stronger sense of community between teachers and students. Supporters of private schools also claim that smaller enrollments give teachers greater opportunities to become acquainted with their students. In turn, this greater familiarity with students allows teachers to better assess each student's strengths and weaknesses, and then tailor instruction to meet individual needs. Consequently, students in private schools consistently score well above the national average.

Most private schools offer programs of instruction that center on some set of shared values. For instance, some schools concentrate on particular subjects, such as the arts or the environment. Others focus on developing their students' character around a shared set of spiritual or religious values. Still others approach character development by emphasizing the importance of social service and social justice. In addition, the values shared by the administration, faculty, and students at private schools can often form a unique sense of community. Some schools may further develop this sense of community by implementing a distinctive teaching method or by requiring students to wear school uniforms. Others, such as residential boarding schools and single-sex institutions, may offer unique social environments.

Private schools often experiment with various aspects of education because they are relatively free of government control. These experiments have produced innovations that have extended throughout all sectors of American education. Since the 1980s, some educators have advanced ideas for public school reform that closely resemble many existing private school practices. These reformers have sought to imitate common features of private education, such as smaller schools and stronger emphasis on academic achievement.

In addition, many educational reformers have sought to change the large bureaucratic management structure of public schools so that it more closely resembles the smaller, school-based management structure of private schools.

Other features include empowering teachers to develop their own curricula, imposing more rigorous academic standards, and reducing class size to provide greater individual attention.

Overall, private schools have a smaller community atmosphere that allows for a lower student-to-teacher ratio, and with smaller class sizes teachers are able to focus more attention on individual students, and have more time to get to know students better. Classmates also get a chance to form more intimate bonds when there are fewer students.

Private schools appear to have fewer disciplinary problems. When teachers and staff know students better, they are able to take appropriate measures applicable to particular students. This works far better than punishing the entire class, which holds no one accountable. The children who behave properly are not motivated to continue good behavior if they are going to be punished for someone else's actions.

Private schools have the option of expulsion which is rare in public schools since public education is considered a "right" rather than a privilege. The possibility of expulsion might make some students less likely to fight, to take drugs, or to cut classes.

When parents pay for their child's education, they enjoy more of the advantage of private schools, because they have a say in how things are done. Parents who voice concerns to public schools frequently complain that the schools treat them as "nuisances." In the private school setting, the parents are paying customers. The tuition factors enable other positives, such as well-maintained campuses, state-of-the-art technology, and excellent books and learning materials.

Many parents who return their children to public school immediately learn that their children are well ahead of their classmates. Many are offered the opportunity to allow their child to skip a grade, because their children have already surpassed what the public school has to offer at their grade level, even in most honors classes, and the students quickly become bored.

Students who receive private schooling also have a lower dropout rate, experience fewer drug problems, and report less violence. They also tend to have higher scores on standardized tests and college entrance exams. By percentage, more private school students go on to college.

Parents, staff, and students alike sing the praises of private schools.

"The mission of my children's school is to strive to serve Christian families by providing an environment of academic quality which is consistent with the Word of God," said Joe, parent of three students attending a private school in Chicago.

"My school prides itself on its ability to give students lots of individual attention and instruction," says the mother of twins attending a small private school in Los Angeles.

"Our parents are required to give a minimum of 25 hours of volunteer service a year," says Ruth, principal at a small Catholic elementary school in St. Petersburg, Florida. "We respect and encourage family and community involvement in the learning process." "When a child sees that their parent is investing in the school as a volunteer, it seems like the child takes more interest in the work that they're doing. It almost becomes like a teamwork thing," said Debbie, a parent at the school and a school board member.

"We believe that all students thrive in a peace-filled spiritual environment where God-given talents and potentials are respected and encouraged," said Jeff, a teacher at a private school in Houston, Texas. "We uphold high expectations for students in citizenship, moral development, the creative process, and academic achievement."

"My school offers a wide variety of creative experiences and activities for children, some that are not offered in the public schools because of budget cuts. We have a state-of-the-art technology program and a Peacemakers program designed to teach students mentoring and conflict-resolution skills," says an administrator at a private middle school in Salem, Oregon.

A Jewish mother praises an academy that offers general Judaic education. "This school believes that 'education' is not just for the children, but something people do throughout their lives. We convey that learning, exploring, and knowing is the goal of the human experience," she says.

A parent in Boston says, "We are offered a wide variety of creative experiences and activities, exciting new extra curricular programs like karate and chess. We are also offered parent education programs to help parents keep up with their children."

A father in Denver says that his child's school is a phenomenal, nurturing atmosphere where his sons are comfortable enough to ask questions about what they are learning. "A teacher told me that education isn't about children finding the right answers, but learning to ask the right questions. I knew immediately this school would turn out to be a gift to my sons."

One parent summed it up, "You only get one shot to give your kids an education. You want it to be the best."

Private school education, whether religious or nonreligious, is all about choice. Children, who look upon these nurturing environments as a second home, are the real beneficiaries.

8

VOUCHERS: THREATENING TO MAKE SCHOOLS IMPROVE

> Victory is won not in miles but in inches. Win a little now, hold your ground, and later, win a little more.
>
> —Louis L'Amour

Most Americans believe that improving our system of education should be a top priority for government at the local, state, and federal levels. Legislators, school boards, educational professionals, parent groups, and community organizations are attempting to implement innovative ideas to rescue children from failing school systems, particularly in inner-city neighborhoods. Many such groups champion voucher programs. The standard program proposed in dozens of states across the country would distribute monetary vouchers (typically valued between $2,500 and $5,000) to parents of school-age children, usually in troubled inner-city school districts. Parents could use the vouchers toward the cost of tuition at private schools, including those dedicated to religious indoctrination.

An educational voucher, commonly called a school voucher, is a certificate by which parents are given the ability to pay for the education of their children at a school of their choice, rather than sending their child to the free public school to which they were assigned. These vouchers would be paid for using tax revenues.

Those in favor of school choice argue that they should be permitted to spend their tax dollars at the educational facility of their choosing, allowing parents to be able to choose which school they want their children to attend. In addition, it is promised that this will allow competition between schools, improving the quality of schools overall. This leads to reduced racial and economic segregation through the abolishment of territorial-based school allocation in the public monopoly system (where students are assigned to schools according to territory, thus dividing students between richer and poorer neighborhoods), as well as a choice of public schools and an improvement in school quality by forcing schools to compete among themselves by offering more diverse and interesting programs.

School vouchers have been in the limelight for over a decade. The basic argument is that giving parents public funds to send their children to private schools will stimulate innovation and competition among schools. Although vouchers lack broad public support, parents in low-income inner cities are more likely to favor alternatives to traditional public education, and this interest has stimulated small pilot programs in several urban school districts.

Such programs have the potential to inform public debate about vouchers' strengths and weaknesses, but they have been evaluated mainly by researchers who openly and actively support vouchers. The media tends to report results from such analysis without the necessary caveats and alternative views. Now that the push for vouchers has reached the federal government, through President Bush's education initiative, the urgency for a balanced perspective has become more important than ever.

Do school vouchers improve academic performance? Voucher advocates claim that students using vouchers improve their academic performance and that the threat of the availability of vouchers leads to improved student performance in public schools.

The idea of public funding of private schools is not new, nor does it belong exclusively to conservative, free market reformers. In the 1960s and early 1970s, educators like Christopher Jencks (1966) argued that vast differences between the quality of public schooling for inner-city blacks and suburban whites could not be resolved within the structure of a segregated public school system. Jencks argued for a policy concept introduced by Milton Friedman (1955) more than a decade earlier. Friedman proposed to offer public funds to families that could be used only for education but in any educational institution, public or private. Such "vouchers" would serve to give families increased choice of the kind of education their children received. Friedman saw vouchers as a way to break the "monopoly" of the public sector over education and increase consumer choice, hence economic welfare. Jencks saw vouchers as a way of improving educational opportunities for a historically discriminated-against group within American society. Both men shared a distrust of the state, Friedman of the bureau-centric state interfering with "democratic" markets and Jencks of the class/race-centric state reproducing inequality through public education.

The voucher issue today has two different political origins. One is a conservative, free-market ideology that prefers private to public provision of any services, and the second is the practical demand of low-income parents for better schooling, public or private. Even if private schools were no more effective than public schools, the market reformers would insist that vouchers make parents and children better off because of choice and competition, and that private school choice should be made available to all parents regardless of income. But the demand in inner cities for better schooling is based not on free-market ideology, but on academic results.

Advocates have been attempting to support two claims: first, that private schools supported by public funds actually can do a better job than public schools of educating children most at risk of school failure, whether because vouchers are a route to smaller classes and better teachers, or because private schools are superior in other respects. Secondly, that vouchers increase incentives for public schools to improve by threatening low-performing public schools with the loss of students to competing private schools.

There have been various programs, with various names, designated for the purpose of using public funds to pay for all or part of the costs of students' tuition at private or religious schools. Proponents of such programs say that they increase "school choice" or "parent choice." Opponents point out that such school choice is limited by the fact that private and religious schools get to choose their students; parents may choose a particular private or religious school but that institution does not have to admit their children. Critics also note that "parent choice" leaves out the rest of the American public, the majority of whom do not have school-age children, who would have no way of knowing how their tax dollars are being used because private and religious schools, unlike public schools, typically do not have to report to the public about how they spend their funds or how well their students are doing academically. The argument continues regarding school choice, vouchers, and student achievement.

There are various types of voucher/tax credit programs now being considered in Congress and state legislatures and we will visit each one below.

Private school vouchers would use taxpayer dollars to pay for all or part of the cost for students to attend private and, often, religious schools. Typically, the money comes out of funds for public schools. Private and religious schools have the option to decide whether or not to participate in various programs. If they choose to participate, they retain the right to decide whether or not to admit a particular voucher student.

Low-income private school vouchers would use taxpayer dollars to pay for all or part of the cost for students from low-income families to attend private, and often, religious schools. Once again, the money comes out of funds for public schools. Private and religious schools have the option to decide whether or not to participate. If they choose to participate, they often retain the right to admit. Some low-income voucher programs may require participating schools to charge voucher students no more than the amount of the voucher. Other programs may allow participating schools to require voucher students to pay the difference between the voucher amount and the school's tuition.

A tuition tax credit is a designated amount of money taxpayers may take as a credit on their state or federal income taxes for expenses associated with sending their children to private or religious schools. The credit may also be available for public school expenses. However, the lion's share of the benefit would go to families who send their children to private or religious schools because their schooling expenses are higher than the educational expenses of families who send their children to public schools. Tuition tax credits are worth more than tuition tax deductions, and they benefit wealthier families more than other families.

A tuition tax deduction is a designated amount of money taxpayers may take as a deduction on their state or federal income taxes for expenses associated with sending their children to private or religious schools and for public school expenses. Tuition tax deductions are of no value to individuals or families who cannot take deductions on their federal or state income taxes (lower-income taxpayers) and thus they benefit wealthier families almost exclusively.

A charitable tuition tax credit is a designated amount of money taxpayers may take as a credit on their state taxes for contributions made to a private school that provides vouchers for students to attend private or religious schools.

An education savings account (K–12) is an investment account, akin to a Roth individual retirement account, where money to pay for public, private, or religious school expenses can be saved. The account provides tax-free earned interest provided it is used for tuition or other educational expenses. Educational savings accounts generally benefit more advantaged families, especially those who already have children in private schools.

School vouchers, also known as scholarships, redirect the flow of educational funding, channeling it directly to individual families rather than to school districts. This allows families to select the public or private schools of their choice and have all or part of the tuition paid. Vouchers are advocated on the grounds that parental choice and competition between public and private schools will improve education for all children. Vouchers can be funded and administered by the government, by private organizations, or by some combination of both.

Voucher programs are very controversial and have been criticized from two very different angles. One body of criticism alleges that competitive markets are not well suited to the field of education and that any school reform based on privatization, competition, and parental choice is doomed to failure. The second body of criticism states that government-funded vouchers would not create a genuinely free educational market, but would perpetuate dependence on government funding and regulation to the continued detriment of certain families.

Some critics of the voucher system note that it is possible to have choice between schools without vouchers. California and Florida districts claim to offer these choices. Other critics argue that given the limited budget for schools, a voucher system weakens public schools while at the same time does not provide enough money for people to attend private schools. A few critics go so far as to say that granting government money to private and religious schools will inevitably lead to increased government control over nongovernment education.

An overwhelming number of critics simply argue that implementation of voucher programs sends a clear message that we are giving up on public education. Sure, vouchers would help *some* students, but the glory of the American system of public education is that it is for *all* students regardless of their religion, academic talents, or their ability to pay a fee. This policy of inclusiveness had made public schools the backbone of American democracy. Private schools are allowed to discriminate on the grounds of low achievement, discipline issues, and sometimes for no reason at all. This is not the American "educational way."

One of my colleagues had this to say: "As our country becomes increasingly diverse, the public school system stands out as an institution that unifies Americans. Under voucher programs, our educational system, and our country, would become even more 'Balkanized' than it already is. With the help of taxpayers' dollars, private schools would be filled with well-to-do and middle-class students and a handful of the best, most motivated students from inner cities. Some public schools would be left with fewer dollars to teach the poorest of the poor and other students who, for one reason or another, were not private school material. Such a scenario can hardly benefit public education."

A wave of bills and referenda have increased the pressure to force local, state, and federal governments to provide subsidies to parents who choose to send their children to private or religious schools instead of free public schools. None of this is new. Nobel Prize–winning economist Milton Friedman proposed such a plan over 60 years ago, but it was received with little enthusiasm.

Today the idea's popularity is spreading across the country, especially among the nation's more conservative elements. Let's take a look at some of the arguments pro and con. First the no votes:

- Voucher students performing the same coursework perform about equally in both public and private schools.

- Why should the public pay to send any child to private school? If private schools wish to have low-income students attend let them offer scholarships.
- Vouchers do not really save money. The cost to taxpayers is extremely high.
- If the public wants private schools to survive, they can donate money or authorize the government to grant special funds. The government does not need to subsidize the education of specific students who attend private schools.
- The playing field is not level. Public schools will become dumping grounds for the unwanted. Private schools are free to pick and choose whomever they wish as students. They do not have to answer to the public and can refuse admission or expel students for any reason.
- Public schools would be robbed of critical funding. Funding of vouchers can cause deep cuts in transportation costs, security, classroom improvements, repairs, supplies, and staff. Inner-city schools could find themselves in even worse situations than they presently are.
- Vouchers subsidize discrimination because private schools are free to refuse or expel any student.
- Bizarre religious groups, political groups, cults, and even profiteers may be allowed to operate schools and receive public money for doing so. Immune from government oversight, they'll be free to pursue whatever gods they may have.
- Private schools will not fix morality. If our children suffer from any moral deficiencies, it is the fault of the parents, not the schools. Inept parents will not find sudden changes in their children just because they attend a private school. The problems facing our nation's youth are difficult and complex and will not simply go away when a student attends a private school.
- Funding religious schools is a violation of the separation of church and state. Religious schools are viewed as extensions of churches.

Those who oppose vouchers conclude that school voucher programs undermine two great traditions: universal public education and the separation of church and state. Instead of embracing vouchers, communities across the country should dedicate themselves to finding solutions that will be available to every American child and then take into account the important legacy of the First Amendment.

So who advocates for voucher programs? Traditionally, support has come from the Catholic Church, an institution that has long maintained the largest system of private religious education in America. Their reasons for saying yes to vouchers are as follows:

- Private schools offer superior education. Many say that math and reading proficiency at private schools is significantly higher than at public schools. These critics go on to say that our nation's publicly run schools are in a state of ruin, failing miserably to properly educate the leaders of tomorrow, and private schools are the only hope for parents who want their children to receive a decent education.
- Vouchers help parents afford an otherwise too expensive education. Presently, only children from wealthy families can afford the benefit of a private education. Publicly funded vouchers would eliminate this unjust disparity and allow for children in low-income homes to get a good education too.
- Vouchers ensure the survival of private schools. Enrollment in private schools declines as the discretionary income of lower and middle-income families declines.
- Overcrowding in public schools would lessen. Public school enrollment all over the country, especially in states like California, New York, and Florida is increasing dramatically and will only get worse. Vouchers can help ease the crisis.
- Competition will force improvement in public schools. Under a free market system, the brightest students will go to the best schools, which are presently private schools. In order to stop such an exodus, public schools will have to do a better job at competing with what private schools offer. Outmoded teaching methods and bloated bureaucracies will have to give way, as they must in free markets.
- Private schools will improve the morals of the nation's youth. Public schools are morally degenerate, failing to provide our youth with proper guidance.

- Voucher programs will not violate the separation of church and state. Voucher programs do not have to force the government to give money to religious schools. The government gives the parents the money, and they, in turn, will be free to give the money to either religious or secular educational institutions. No money will be transferred directly from government to churches.

As voucher advocates and opponents debate and litigate, vouchers continue to receive attention within presidential debates, think tanks, and academic conferences. We all know that since 1960, test scores and other measures of achievement have taken a downward spiral even though spending on elementary and high schools has more than quadrupled. In most inner cities, the schools resemble prisons and the crime rate on school property approaches that of the neighborhood at large. Teachers' unions, backed by the bureaucratic establishment, go ballistic any time reforms are suggested that threaten the status quo. The intellectual marketplace has been ripe for new ideas that complement these reforms.

Parents, with the help of educational reformers and a few politicians, have pushed through a number of voucher initiatives. The most noteworthy are in Milwaukee and Cleveland. Both offer tuition vouchers to several thousand low-income students.

Milwaukee has more than 15 years of experience with vouchers, with approximately 10,000 children receiving public dollars in order to attend private schools. Whenever anyone comes up with a new voucher plan, they inevitably come to Milwaukee, long considered "ground zero" in the voucher movement. Milwaukee began its voucher program in 1990, Cleveland began a similar program in 1995, and Florida started a small statewide program in 1999.

Milwaukee's private voucher schools receive public tax dollars, yet get to operate by different rules than public schools. Under Milwaukee's program, voucher schools do not have to administer the statewide tests required of public schools or any assessments if they choose not to. These schools do not have to release data such as test scores, attendance, racial breakdown of students, suspensions, or dropout rates.

Milwaukee has gone beyond these two points and has provided data to show success. Educational opportunities for African American,

Latino, and other low-income students have led to increased academic performance. Milwaukee has found a way to give low-income blacks and Latinos the same chance as middle-class whites to choose a private school. Cleveland follows the same pattern.

Nobel laureate Milton Friedman, who invented vouchers, advocates making vouchers available to all parents who remove their children from public schools. His original idea was to provide any student who left a public school with a voucher equal in value to the average amount spent per pupil by the local school district. In the intervening years he has modified his position slightly, arguing that the private sector should be able to provide schooling for less than the government. He now thinks that vouchers valued at about half the per-pupil expenditure would be sufficient to entice private schools to accept students from public schools.

From the start Friedman has argued that the government's monopoly on schools could be challenged only if private schools had more clout. He invented vouchers as a mechanism to generate funding for religious schools or secular schools operated by nonprofit organizations.

Friedman has also been very vocal about opposing what he calls "welfare vouchers," arguing that they separate individuals because of their incomes. He reasserts that as long as public schooling remains an entitlement, tuition vouchers should be considered a form of tax relief. Friedman believes that people of all income levels are entitled to get some of their taxes back if they relieve the government of the burden of providing schooling for their children.

The Institute for Justice often defends voucher programs in court, arguing that even low-income programs should entice entrepreneurs to create schools that would serve students bearing tuition vouchers. A voucher system could rescue impoverished students from violence-ridden inner-city schools and break the death grip of teachers' unions and powerful administrators on public-school governance. The institute goes on to say that the fate of vouchers will be decided in the courts.

Along with Ohio and Wisconsin, Vermont has its own voucherlike program, called tuitioning. In Vermont, those towns that are too small to finance a public school let their school-aged children attend private schools. The town's taxpayers pay at least part of the tuition.

All three state's voucher plans have been taken to court by civil liberties groups and teachers' unions, citing the First Amendment's Establishment Clause to challenge the use of vouchers to subsidize students who want to attend religious schools. The Institute of Justice has represented parents in all three states, hoping to establish a precedent that would allow any school to accept vouchers.

Teachers' unions have been the institute's most vocal opponents in court. The National Education Association (NEA) and its state affiliates have thrown time, money, and expertise into opposing every educational reform that would inject competitive pressures into schooling, including merit pay.

Vouchers may not win often at the ballot box or in the state legislature but they are remaining useful as a threat to the educational establishment. Milwaukee gets a lot of attention because nearly 2,000 low-income students receive tuition vouchers as well as over 5,000 difficult-to-educate students. At least 17 states provide tax funding to educate at-risk students privately. Houston had over 5,000 students who could not attend their neighborhood schools because of overcrowding. These students were given vouchers to attend private schools.

On June 27, 2002, the U.S. Supreme Court decided to uphold school vouchers. Many hoped that this decision, in taking up whether Cleveland's voucher program violated the separation of church and state, would settle the contentious issue of public dollars for private religious schools. The court decision was a serious blow to supporters of public education and a boon to the voucher movement.

However, the stumbling blocks remain. These have always been policy issues such as money accountability and whether vouchers undercut effort to improve public schools.

Opponents cite an accountability issue. Private voucher schools do not have to adhere to basic requirements such as release of records on academic achievement while public schools are being forced to take an even broader array of tests to prove academic effectiveness. The voucher schools are exempt from testing. Even if they choose to give these tests they still do not have to release the results. In Milwaukee, after spending more than $200 million on the program, the public has no data on the academic performance of their voucher students.

Clearly, the voucher movement has gained political support because it targets low-income families and is sympathetic to African American and Latino families in urban areas. Just as clearly, the strategic goal of the voucher movement is universal vouchers. Most predictions are that voucher supporters will move incrementally, proposing targeted programs until they gather enough political support to make a frontal assault and call for universal vouchers. Voucher supporters are currently hoping to please both sides by pushing low-income vouchers in some areas and tuition tax credits in others.

Many educators believe that the threat of vouchers motivates schools to improve. A study of Florida's efforts to turn around failing schools has found that the threat that children would receive vouchers to attend private schools spurred the worst performing schools to make significant academic strides.

Jay P. Greene of the Manhattan Institute, a research group based in downtown Manhattan, conducted the study, sponsored by the Florida Department of Education. The stakes are high. Florida's educational program has been held up as a model for its combination of aggressive testing of school performance and its backing by taxpayer-financed vouchers.

The study by Greene found that 76 public schools in Florida that had received failing scores on the state achievement test once, and would have lost children to private schools if they failed a second time, all improved enough to remove themselves from the failing list in the course of the second year. The most obvious explanation for these findings is that an accountability system with vouchers as the sanction for repeated failure really motivates schools to improve.

The reforming idea behind vouchers is that parents would enjoy freedom of choice in the market of schools. Educators would compete for as many vouchers as possible by offering the best education possible. Schools that lost too many "customers" would go bankrupt and be replaced by better ones. Supporters claim that this retains the best of both worlds. All students, regardless of their class or race, could still receive a publicly funded education, but they would also benefit as consumers in a competitive market that ostensibly produces the highest quality of education at the lowest cost.

Some say voucher proponents have a larger agenda: the public financing of religious education, and the eventual elimination of public education entirely.

It is only fair to allow critics to argue the flaws of the voucher system. They keep saying that vouchers do not work and that no academic improvement is shown. They also say that there is a question of space. In California, a survey found that there was no space in private schools to accommodate public schoolchildren wishing to attend. This problem is compounded by the fact that the better the reputation of the private school, the less they need to take voucher students. Many claim that vouchers will stratify education and society. Vouchers would stratify schools by income, class, race, and religion. Public schools currently serve as America's melting pot where children from all walks of life grow together. They learn that diversity is normal. Diversity opens up intellectual horizons where different voices bring new viewpoints, challenge people to look at things in new ways, and point out the errors of single-mindedness. So how would vouchers kill diversity? By the so-called freedom of choice option. Freedom of choice is a misnomer and a euphemism. What vouchers actually offer is freedom to exclude, and only those with money or power can exercise this option. The poor are not free to choose a private school that costs more than the value of the voucher. They are forced to accept whatever school they can afford. Parents have little choice in this matter. Private schools select their students for their high academic achievement or membership in a select social group. Low-achieving public school students don't stand much of a chance of being accepted into private schools seeking academically superior students. In Milwaukee the best private schools simply declined to participate in the program.

Vouchers allow schools to escape accountability. Vouchers upset the balance between parental and public control over education. Vouchers are at the center of the controversy of who should control a child's education, parents or society? These critics say that on an instinctive level, parental control makes sense. After all the parents gave birth to the child, they care the most and want to raise the child they best way they can. However, parental concern is far different from knowing what is best for the child. They use the analogy that when a child gets sick the parent seeks medical advice, they don't attempt to cure them. With regard to education, the parent cannot possibly know about every subject. Public schools serve society and create social cohesion by creating a common language and culture and a shared body of knowledge. Therefore, choose the public school system.

The school voucher issue remains controversial. It has come to the forefront of political, societal, constitutional, and economic discourse.

Proponents say vouchers promote school choice. This gives all parents the choice to be integral participants in their child's education. Power and choices make people feel more involved, more effective, and more satisfied as citizens. Children whose parents make choices learn better. It's about improving public education, better preparing students for college or the workforce. It's about equality, empowerment, and children. Opponents cite economic issues, societal issues, and constitutional issues previously touched on. Proponents point out cases that suggest vouchers enhance educational performance, while opponents analyze the same cases using different statistics and studies that suggest the opposite. You must decide.

Educational reformers are in the midst of a fierce debate over school vouchers and the future of public education in the United States, but the American people haven't joined them yet. It isn't just that the people are undecided as much as they are unaware. The vast majority of the public knows very little about school vouchers, charter schools, or for-profit schools. This lack of familiarity extends to both parents and nonparents, ordinary citizens and local civic leaders, and cuts across all lines of geography and demographics. With minor differences, it even extends to parents in areas where vouchers have been in place for some time.

Of course, it's quite common to find that the general public has less technical information on an issue than experts and policy makers. Often, however, the public has a firm grasp of the values that underlie a policy option. In the case of vouchers, educators found that even the concept of using free market competition to improve schools was unfamiliar to most people. This does not mean that the public is satisfied with the current system or rejects the idea of vouchers. But most people are quite open in admitting they need to know more before making a decision.

The public's lack of focus does not mean that people don't care about how this debate is resolved or that their concerns do not merit consideration. In fact, I believe this is a challenging job for leaders in education, politics, and the news media in order to bring the debate to communities and families nationwide. This is no small task, and it is of fundamental importance. I hope that those who recognize the public's stake in the voucher debate are willing to "walk the extra mile" to invite the American people to join in.

9

DISTANCE LEARNING: THE WAVE OF THE FUTURE

Everything you can imagine is real.

—Pablo Picasso

Andre is 16-years-old and is a new father. Three weeks after the baby was born his girlfriend handed his son over to him and walked out of his life. He has no idea where she is. Andre had been living on the streets and has no contact with his parents. He has never met his dad and has not seen his mother in several months. Determined to care for his son, Andre found a minimum-wage job in a local grocery store sweeping up and stocking shelves for 8 hours a day. He rents a room above the store, and the owner's wife takes care of his son, for a price. There is no way Andre could go to school. A customer told Andre about Distance Learning. "This saved my life," said Andre. "Now I can keep my job, support my son, and finish my education."

What is distance education? Within the context of rapid technological change and shifting market conditions, the American educational system is challenged with providing increased educational opportunities without increasing costs. Many educational institutions are answering this challenge by developing distance education. At its most basic level, distance education takes place when a teacher and students are separated by physical distance, and technology (voice, video, data, and print), often in concert with face-to-face communication, is used to bridge the instructional gap. These types of programs can provide students with a second chance at education; reach those disadvantaged by limited time, distance, or physical disability; and update the knowledge base of workers at their places of employment.

Is distance education effective? Many educators ask if distance students can learn as much as students receiving traditional face-to-face instruction. When the method and technology used are appropriate to the instructional tasks, when there is student-to-student interaction, and when there is timely teacher-to-student feedback, teaching and studying at a distance can be as effective as traditional instruction.

How is distance education delivered? Wide ranges of technological options are available to the distance educator, such as voice, video, data, and print. Instructional audio tools include the interactive technologies of telephone, audio conferencing, and shortwave radio. Instructional video tools include still images such as slides; preproduced moving images such as film; and videotape and real-time moving images, combined with audio conferencing, one-way or two-way video, and two-way audio.

Another technological option is data. Computers send and receive information electronically. For this reason, the term *data* is used to describe this broad category of instructional tools. Computer applications for distance education are varied and include computer assisted instruction (CAI), which uses the computer as a self-contained teaching machine to present individual lessons, and computer managed instruction (CMI), which uses the computer to organize/instruct and track student records and progress. The instruction itself need not be delivered via a computer, although CAI is often combined with CMI. Computer mediated education (CME) describes computer applications that facilitate the delivery of instruction. Examples include electronic mail, fax, computer conferencing, and World Wide Web applications.

Print is a foundational element of distance education programs and the basis from which all other delivery systems have evolved. Various print formats are available including textbooks, study guides, workbooks, course syllabi, and case studies.

Which technology is best? Although technology plays a key role in the delivery of distance education, educators must remain focused on instructional outcomes, not the technology of delivery. The key to effective distance education is focusing on the needs of the learners, the requirements of the content, and the constraints faced by the teacher, before selecting a delivery system. Typically, this systematic approach will result in a mix of media, each serving a specific purpose. For example, a strong print component can provide much of the basic instructional content in the form of a course text, as well as readings, the syllabus, and a day-to-day schedule. Interactive audio or video conferencing can provide real time face-to-face or voice-to-voice interaction. This is also an excellent and cost-effective way to incorporate guest speakers and content experts. Computer conferencing or electronic mail can be used to send messages, assignment feedback, and other targeted communication to one or more class members. It can also be used to increase interaction among students. Prerecorded video tapes can be used to present class lectures and visually oriented content. Fax can be used to distribute assignments and last minute announcements, to receive student assignments, and to provide timely feedback.

Using this integrated approach, the educator's task is to carefully select among the technological options. The goal is to build a mix of instructional media, meeting the needs of the learner in a manner that is instructionally effective and economically prudent.

What is effective distance education? Without exception, effective distance education programs begin with careful planning and focused understanding of course requirements and student needs. Appropriate technology can only be selected once these elements are understood in detail. There is no mystery to the way effective distance education programs develop. They don't happen spontaneously, they evolve through the hard work and dedicated efforts of many individuals and organizations. In fact, successful distance education programs rely on the consistent and integrated efforts of students, faculty, facilitators, support staff, and administrators.

Who are the key players in distance education? The following briefly describes the roles of the key players in the distance education enterprise and the challenges they face.

Students. Meeting the instructional needs of students is the cornerstone of every effective distance education program, and the test by which all efforts in the field are judged. Regardless of the educational context, the primary role of the student is to learn. This is a daunting task under the best of circumstances, requiring motivation, planning, and an ability to analyze and apply the instructional content being taught. When instruction is delivered from a distance, additional challenges result because students are often separated from classmates who may share their backgrounds and interests, have few if any opportunities to interact with teachers outside of class, and must rely on technical linkages to bridge the gap separating class participants.

Faculty. The success of any distance education effort rests squarely on the shoulders of the faculty. In a traditional classroom setting, the instructor's responsibility includes assembling course content and developing an understanding of student needs. Special challenges confront those teaching from a distance. For example, the instructor must develop an understanding of the characteristics and needs of distance learners with little first-hand experience and limited, if any, face-to-face contact; adapt his or her teaching style, taking into consideration the needs and expectations of multiple, often diverse audiences; develop a working understanding of delivery technology, while remaining focused on their teaching role; and be able to function effectively as a skilled facilitator as well as content provider.

Facilitators. The instructor often finds it beneficial to rely on a site facilitator to act as a bridge between the students and the instructor. To be effective, a facilitator must understand the students being served and the instructor's expectations. Most importantly, the facilitator must be willing to follow the directions established by the teacher. Where budget and logistics permit, the role of on-site facilitator has increased even in classes in which they have little, if any, content expertise. At a minimum, they set up equipment, collect assignments, proctor tests, and act as the instructor's on-site eyes and ears.

Support staff. These individuals are the silent heroes of the distance education enterprise who must deal effectively with the myriad details required for program success. Most successful distance education programs consolidate support service functions, such as student registration materials, duplication and distribution, textbook ordering, securing of copyright clearances, scheduling, processing grade reports, managing technical resources, and so forth. Support personnel are truly the glue that keeps the distance education effort together and on track.

Administrators. Although administrators are typically influential in planning an institution's distance education program, they often lose contact or relinquish control to technical management once the program is operational. Effective distance education administrators are more than idea people. They are consensus builders, decision makers, and referees. They work closely with technical service personnel, ensuring that technological resources are effectively deployed to further the institution's academic mission. Most importantly, they maintain an academic focus, realizing that meeting the instructional needs of distance students is their ultimate responsibility.

What is different about distance teaching? Classroom teachers rely on a number of visual and unobtrusive cues from their students to enhance their delivery of instructional content. A quick glance reveals who is attentively taking notes, pondering a difficult concept, or preparing to make a comment. The student who is frustrated, confused, tired, or bored is equally evident. The attentive teacher consciously and subconsciously receives and analyzes these visual cues and adjusts the course delivery to meet the needs of the class during a particular lesson.

In contrast, the distant teacher has fewer, if any, visual cues. Those cues that do exist are filtered through technological devices such as video monitors. It is difficult to carry on a stimulating teacher and class discussion when spontaneity is altered by technical requirements and distance.

Without the use of a real-time visual medium such as television, the teacher receives no visual information from the distance site. The teacher might never really know if a student is asleep, talking, or even in the room. Separation by distance also affects the rapport of the class. Living in different communities, geographic regions, or even states, deprives the teachers and students of a common community link.

Why teach from a distance? Many teachers feel the opportunities offered by distance education outweigh the obstacles. In fact, instructors often comment that the focused preparation required by distance teaching improved their overall teaching and empathy for their students. The challenges posed by distance education are countered by opportunities to reach a wider student audience, meet the needs of students who are unable to attend classes, involve outside speakers who would otherwise be unavailable, and link students from different social, cultural, economic, and experiential backgrounds.

Planning and organizing a distance-learning program is very important to the well-being of the student. In developing or adapting distance instruction, the core content remains basically unchanged, although its preparation requires new strategies and additional preparation time. Suggestions for planning and organizing a distance-delivered course include looking at distance education research findings, reviewing the existing programs for content and materials, presenting the format, and analyzing and understanding the strengths and weaknesses of the possible delivery systems available (audio, video, data, and print) in terms of student needs.

In addition, what types of hands-on training are necessary for technology use must be determined, and the delivery of the program must be based on the type of technology available. Consider a preclass session in which the class meets informally to learn about the delivery system and the responsibility of the tech support staff. The teacher should initiate a frank discussion and set the rules, guidelines, and start date for the program. Once procedures are in place, the teacher should uphold them consistently.

Parents and prospective students need to make sure each site is equipped with functional and accessible equipment. Ask if course materials are to be sent by mail, and if so, check for deadlines and assurance that they will arrive well before the first class begins.

What is the profile of the distance-learning student? The primary role of the student is to learn. Under the best of circumstances, this challenging task requires motivation, planning, and the ability to analyze and apply the information being taught in a distance-education setting. The process of student learning is more complex for several reasons. Many distance-education students are older (17–21), have outside jobs, and even families. They must coordinate different areas of their lives, which influence each other (family, job, studies). Many distance students also have a variety of reasons for taking the course (pursuing graduation, making up missed class credits, learning new job skills, etc.).

In distance education, the learner is usually isolated. The motivational factors arising from contact or competition with other students is absent. The student also lacks the immediate support of an on-site teacher, who is able to motivate and, if necessary, give attention to their needs and difficulties that crop up during study.

Distance students and their teacher often have little in common in terms of background and day-to-day experiences, and therefore, it takes longer for student-teacher rapport to develop. Without face-to-face contact, distance students may feel ill at ease with their teacher as an individual and become uncomfortable with their learning situation.

If you are to become a distance learner, remember that technology is the conduit through which information and communication flow. Until the teacher and student become comfortable with the delivery system used, communication will be inhibited.

Beginning students may have some difficulty determining what the demands of a course of academic study actually are because they do not have the support of an immediate peer group, ready access to the instructor, or familiarity with the technology being used for delivery. They may become unsure of themselves and how to learn the material. Students who are not confident about their learning tend to concentrate on memorizing facts and details in order to complete assignments and write exams. As a result, they end up with a poor understanding of the course material.

Distance learners need to become more selective and focused in their learning in order to master new information. Students need to be able to relate and distinguish new ideas and previous knowledge, relate concepts to everyday experience, relate and distinguish evidence and argument, organize content, and focus on how instructional material relates to everyday life.

Distance students, no matter what age, must first become responsible for themselves. Teachers can help motivate by providing consistent feedback, encouraging discussion among students, and reinforcing effective student study habits. Students need to learn their own strengths, desires, skills, and needs.

Distance learners also need to maintain and even increase their self-esteem. Student performance is enhanced with family support and timely teacher feedback. Students learn most effectively when they can relate to and interact with other students. When students are unable to meet together, appropriate interactive technology should be provided to encourage small group and individual communication.

Distance students need to reflect on what they have learned, are learning, and still need to learn. They need to examine their existing knowledge frameworks and reflect on how they can be added to or changed by incoming information.

How does distance learning meet student needs? To function effectively, students must quickly become comfortable with the nature of teaching and learning at a distance. Teachers should make sure to adapt the delivery system to best meet the needs of the students, in terms of both content and preferred learning styles. Consider the following strategies teachers may use for meeting students' needs: assisting the students to become both familiar and comfortable with the delivery technology, preparing them to resolve the technical problems that will arise, and focusing on joint problem solving and not placing blame for occasional technical difficulties. If things change during the course, teachers should try to make the students aware and comfortable with new patterns of communication that may be used. Teachers should always learn about their student's backgrounds and experiences, and discussing their own background and interests is equally important. Teachers must be sensitive to different communication styles and varied cultural backgrounds, remembering that students may have different language skills. And, students need to take an active role in the distance-delivered course by independently taking responsibility for their learning.

Teachers who are teaching distance courses should try to develop effective teaching skills. For the most part, effective distance teaching requires the enhancement of existing skills rather than developing new abilities. Teachers should pay special attention to assessing the amount of content that can be effectively delivered in the course. Presenting content at a distance usually takes more time than presenting the same content in a traditional classroom. Teachers should diversify and pace course activities and avoid long lectures. Content presentation should be interspersed with discussions and student-centered exercises, with attention to student learning styles. Teachers can humanize the course by focusing on the student, not the delivery system. Locally relevant case studies and examples and concise, direct questions should be used, allowing for increased time for response due to technological linkages. Strategies for student reinforcement, review, repetition, and remediation should be developed. One-on-one phone discussions and electronic mail communication can be used. Finally, teachers can relax and let their students grow comfortable with the process of distance education.

Using effective interaction and feedback strategies will enable the instructor to identify and meet individual student needs while providing a forum for suggesting course improvements. To improve interaction and feedback, teachers should consider the following:

- Use preclass study questions to encourage critical thinking on the part of all learners.
- Require early contact and interaction via e-mail.
- Arrange telephone office hours as well as evening hours for those who work.
- Use a variety of delivery systems (conference calls, e-mail, video, computers, etc.).
- Contact each student at least weekly.
- Have students keep a journal of their thoughts and ideas regarding the course, their individual progress, and other concerns. Have students submit the journals frequently.
- Use an on-site facilitator to stimulate interaction.
- Make detailed comments on written assignments. Return assignments without delay, using fax or electronic mail.

Evaluation is a critical piece of distance learning. In these programs, students and parents are assured that teachers use a variety of means, some formal and some informal, to determine how much and how well their students are learning. To formally evaluate student learning, most teachers use quizzes, tests, examinations, term papers, lab reports, and homework. These formal evaluation techniques allow instructors to evaluate student achievement and assign grades.

To evaluate classroom learning informally, teachers pose questions, listen carefully to student questions and comments, and monitor body language and facial expressions. Informal, often implicit evaluations permit the teachers to make adjustments in their teaching, to slow down or review material in response to questions, confusion, misunderstanding, or to move on when student performance exceeds expectations.

When teaching from a distance, educators must address a different teaching challenge than when teaching in a traditional classroom. There is no longer a familiar classroom setting, a homogeneous group of students, face-to-face feedback, or convenient opportunities to speak with students one-on-one.

Distance educators may find it useful to find an approach that shows student comfort with the method used to deliver the distant learning instruction, the appropriateness of assignments, the clarity of course content, if class time is well spent, and teaching effectiveness.

Evaluation can be formative, summative, or a combination of both. Formative evaluation is an ongoing process to be considered at all stages of instruction that will enable the instructor to improve the course as he or she proceeds. Postcards to share concerns, electronic mail, and the telephone are great ways to communicate.

Summative evaluation assesses the overall effectiveness of the finished product of the course and can be a baseline for designing a new plan, program, or course, and for revising a current course.

What to evaluate is equally important. Teachers should consider evaluating the use of technology, class formats and environment, course content, assignments, tests, support services, student achievement, and student attitude. Above all, teachers need to establish rapport with their students by being interested and supportive and to solicit both positive and negative feedback to learn what is not working as well as what is working.

Students in distance-learning programs are successful. Why? Many of the students are highly motivated and self-disciplined. They are serious about the courses offered, willing to call teachers for assistance, and have their priorities in order. Many students have families; they may be pregnant teens who want to continue their education, or are new parents with more time constraints. Instruction appears to be successful and interaction is important.

Perhaps the question educational institutions must answer is whether part of their mission as educators is to offer programs to those who might not be reached without distance education. The primary benefit of distance education to educational institutions is the increased number of nontraditional students they are able to attract and serve.

How do I go about choosing a school for my child's needs? Before you enroll your child in online classes, take a few minutes to interview the school of your choice. Asking questions up front can ensure that the school is a perfect match. The following are suggestions of what to ask as you look into a distance-learning program:

- Is this school accredited?
- Are there any hidden fees or costs?
- What education and experience do the teachers have?
- How many students does each teacher work with?
- What hardware and software is required?
- How long does it take to complete a course program?
- Can I speed ahead or work at my own pace?
- What curriculum is used?
- Am I expected to work independently or can I get extra help?
- How long has the school existed? (The longer the better, experience is a plus.)
- How many students are currently enrolled?
- How many students have graduated from the program?
- How do I find a distance-learning charter school in my area?

Enrolling in a distance-learning charter school is a respectable and free way to earn a high school diploma from home. A charter school is a state-funded institution that has more control of its programs than traditional public schools. Charter schools often experiment with nontraditional methods of teaching and learning.

Many states now offer distance-learning charter school programs for elementary, middle, and high school students. Distance-learning charter school programs are held over the Internet or through the mail. Oftentimes, a student is assigned a teacher who makes home visits on a weekly or monthly basis. Because charter schools are a public service, the state pays for all textbooks and course material and may even cover the cost of computer hardware, software, and a home Internet connection.

Are you interested in enrolling your child in a distance-learning charter school? Here is what you need to do to find out what schools exist in your community: Step one is to find out if your state even has distance-learning charter schools. Check out state-by-state information at the US Charter School's website (www.uscharterschools.org). Check the individual state charter websites. Step two is to search for the program that fits your child best. Step three is to identify the schools that your child qualifies for. Some states require that distance-learning students live in the same district or area that their charter school operates in. One school may only admit students from their local district.

Another may enroll students from a large portion of the state. Step four is to evaluate the schools that your child qualifies for. Not all charter schools are equal. Try to find a program that is well established, will meet your child's needs, and has a high student satisfaction rate. Talking with parents, teachers, and students before enrolling your child can help put your mind at ease.

Distance learning is a viable part of our educational system today, and is here to stay. Teaching and learning from a distance is demanding. Learning will be more meaningful and "deeper" for distance students if the students and their instructor share responsibility for developing learning goals and objectives; actively interacting with class members; promoting reflection on experience; relating new information to examples that make sense to learners; maintaining self-esteem; and evaluating what is being learned. This is the challenge and the opportunity provided by distance education.

10

TEACHER/STUDENT/PARENT ATTRACTION

No one can force change on anyone else. It has to be experienced. Unless we invent ways where paradigm shifts can be experienced by large numbers of people, then change will remain a myth.

—Eric Trist

TEACHERS

Elvin is an energetic boy. He is small for 5 years old, but he has the whirlwind energy of someone on a mission. He lives in the projects two blocks from an alternative elementary school where he is in Bobbie Sue's kindergarten class. He lives with his mother and three older brothers, and these days Elvin is flying high because he knows he is going to college. He knows because Bobbie Sue told him so. She told Elvin that if he keeps practicing his reading the way he has been, nothing would stand in his way. Elvin has been working on reading as part of the school's year-long reading campaign. Every night he takes home a piece of paper that says, "I am a Reader Leader," and asks his mother to read with him for 20 minutes. When she does, she signs off on the form and Elvin brings it back to school. He has had perfect compliance since the program began. If he can maintain that record, he'll become an official Reader Leader and win prizes: a neat blue water bottle from a local bank, a basketball from the Minnesota Timberwolves, and a chance to go to a concert and magic show featuring Pearl Jam. Elvin's mother likes the program too. She says that she really enjoys the quiet time they have together, those reading minutes are some of the nicest moments in her day.

Teachers like Bobbie Sue make a difference. Ineffective teachers are boring, unprepared, or unable to maintain discipline in even the best classes. Successful teachers do best when they have freedom to express themselves, to improvise, and to manage discipline. The trademark of a successful teacher is often an unconventional approach to teaching. For example, one California charter schoolteacher, Maria, illustrates the concept of inertia (the tendency of a moving body to remain in motion) by gliding around her classroom on roller skates.

One parent had this to say: "My son was going to drop out of school. He felt like a failure, and he had closed his mind to learning. Then he found a teacher who cared. The going was rough but his teacher hung in there. He found ways to help him learn, think, and succeed. Without his teacher, he would have been one of those statistics where everyone wonders what went wrong. I will be forever grateful to him and the other teachers who worked long hours to provide a rich, nurturing, safe, and engaging environment for my son."

Today's schools face enormous challenges. In response to an increasingly complex society and a rapidly changing technology-based economy, schools are being asked to educate the most diverse student body in our history to higher academic standards then ever before. The task is one that cannot be "teacher proofed" through management systems, testing mandates, or curriculum packages. Programs are being designed in which teachers show deep understanding of subject content and are flexible enough to help students create cognitive maps, relate ideas to one another, and address misconceptions. Teachers are connecting ideas across fields and to everyday life. They are teaching in ways that connect with students as well as forming a foundation that includes understanding differences that may arise from school, family experiences, and learning styles.

Teachers are speaking out for change. This country's public schools employ many talented, committed educators. Unfortunately, these excellent teachers are frustrated by a system that does not value their skills.

Teachers report that they are choosing to teach in alternative schools because of the philosophy of the school, the smaller class sizes, and the fact that they have more authority and a less stifling bureaucracy. Teachers also say that their job is to help individual students to clarify their aspirations, to develop plans for step-by-step attainment of those aspirations, to monitor students' progress, and then to try to understand and alleviate the problems students encounter. The faculty maintains a climate of high expectations in academic achievement and maintains an interdisciplinary dialogue that helps prevent students from "falling through the cracks."

Strategies of teaching must be grounded in an understanding of students' unique multiple identities and communities. Teaching about and from the cultures of the students is more than a political statement. It is sound educational theory. Students construct knowledge by incorporating new understanding with the background that they bring into the classroom.

A command of the subject matter, such that the students pick up on the teacher's excitement about it, is fundamental. Phil's incredible knowledge of the tropical fish found in the tanks in his apartment or his description of what his snake ate for dinner is meaningful to his students, especially since his students have been to his apartment to view the fish tanks and the snake. Bruce's leading questions about social issues are opening the student's mind up for learning, making the students more engaged. Both teachers are allowing their students to see the world differently.

Caring deeply about the students' accomplishments and growth is equally important. Teachers must recognize the student as an individual who brings particular experience, interests, enthusiasm, and fears into the classroom. When the teacher takes time to acknowledge a student's life outside the classroom, relationships develop.

When teachers visit the neighborhood organizations that their students attend, they begin to build connections between the community and the classroom. For instance, a high school English teacher in California saw one of her low-achieving students in an entirely new light when she watched him star in a play at the community theater. In

Pennsylvania, an English teacher visited a church-based literacy project and saw several of his students researching and writing for the church newsletter in ways he had not seen in his classroom, and he revised his writing curriculum to make the most of their after-school experience.

Teachers do what is best for their students. I believe that the single most significant decision I can make on a day-to-day basis is my choice of attitude. It is more important than my past, my education, my bankroll, my successes or failures, fame or pain, what other people think of me or say about my circumstances, my position, or me. I have learned that making a conscious effort to have a positive attitude is an important prerequisite to success with my students.

Beliefs determine behavior. What we sow is what we reap. We get what we settle for. For whatever reason, maybe self-esteem, many students need the structure of a positive attitude first provided by the teacher. In their lives of turmoil, students are easily influenced by factors and attitudes outside of themselves. A teacher can use this fact to expect higher levels of behavior and work performances. If you enter the classroom with the attitude that the students are thugs who do not want to learn, that is what you will get. We can script our students for behaviors, good or bad. All students will rise to your level of expectations.

Bond with your students, catch them being good, and instill them with a positive school experience. Be caring and trusting and avoid power struggles. Power does not influence. If a teacher uses power or control, a student will do one of three things: submit, fight, or withdraw (often leading to dropping out).

Adopt the "I want you back when you're ready" policy. Let the student know that the behavior is not acceptable but also allow students to save face in front of their peers. Come on strong and students will fight back. De-escalate the power struggle, disarm, and watch them come to you.

Alternative schools appear to make learning seem easy. These schools fit into the child's rhythm and give them what they need. Our style, dress, and demeanor contribute to success, or lack thereof, with students. Since students spend more time with their teachers than with parents, teachers are a big influence on their lives.

Learning is greatly increased if the student has a need. Teaching is ineffective if the student does not feel a need to learn. Instead of trying to change the students, we need to change the way we teach them.

A lot of stress and ineffective teaching comes into play when all students are expected to be doing the same thing at the same time. Alternative schools offer a combination of individualized instruction with cooperative learning. Students are often grouped together on similar content. For example, this might mean four different cooperative groups in a classroom working on four different assignments. Each groups' members may also change from day to day. Flexibility becomes the key.

If teachers keep being positive with kids, even though they don't get any feedback, what they do will always be remembered somewhere. Keep trying, keep hustling, and keep the positive energy flowing. Be the teacher students will want to come to and emulate.

Teachers who work in alternative schools quickly realize that the core of classroom discipline is really a teacher's well-planned curriculum, the implementation of that curriculum, and the integration of each lesson with the overall aims of the course. If a teacher has the curriculum organized and is excited about teaching it, he or she is on the way. If the students like you, it is an added plus. If students don't like you, or sense that you don't like them, they will do their best to make life hell on earth for you. Establish good rapport and you will have students on your side.

Some of our larger public schools are run like factories or jails and the students are treated like prisoners. Remember, schools exist to serve the students.

There is currently a gap between the needs of today's students and what society and schools are providing. We are often handed a lot of "half-raised" kids. Therefore, a large part of what we do for our students is to give them a sense of hope. The greatest gift we can give someone is to open their eyes to their own greatness; to the potential they never knew existed. We also need to instill in our students the idea that it is okay to fail, but it is not okay to give up. We need to teach our students that difficulty, frustration, and failure are a normal part of the learning process.

The hallway in your school may be dreary and old. The paint may be chipping off the walls because there is not enough money to make repairs. Graffiti may be visible and you may look out the windows of a school built almost 100 years ago. Your footsteps may echo down the hall. Now you have a choice. In your mind you can make that school a painful place to be or a place filled with passion. You can consider the conditions and get depressed or become excited about the challenge.

You can be a powerful influence and a model for young minds to follow if you choose. You are dealing with young people who are at a fork in the road of life. It is up to us to promote positive choices. When you walk into the classroom you will see faces full of pain, hope, fear, apprehension, and excitement. These are kids often living for the now, but inside longing to be accepted and to become successful. Make your students believe they can do it. Give them the best you can. Be the best that you can. If you make just one person breathe easier, you have done an enormous human service. You, the students, and society will benefit. Remember that "luck" is preparation meeting opportunity. I hope you have the opportunity to touch some lives forever.

Teachers in alternative educational settings have developed the following characteristics that are crucial for effectively teaching alternative students:

- A teacher must have high expectations.
- A teacher should show intense personal warmth in combination with a demand for a high level of achievement expressed as personal concern for the student.
- A teacher should use democratic practices in the classroom so that the teacher and student are united in planning, organizing, implementing, and participating in their common activities.
- A teacher should use a combination of firmness and kindness and indirect criticism and humor.
- A teacher is a model that sets the stage for learning, acceptance, and respect.
- Teachers are motivated by time to work with other teachers and meaningful professional development.
- Teachers are developing a culture of face-to-face and data-driven accountability.
- Teachers who work in school-choice settings have developed instructional strategies that have been shown to increase academic achievement.

Define instructional expectations (learning objectives, procedures used to achieve them, and criteria used to judge their achievement). These need to be spelled out before instruction begins.

- Take student readiness into account.
- Provide accurate evaluation of student performance.
- Utilize repetition effectively as well as recall of information.
- Communicate clearly.
- Facilitate teamwork and cooperative learning.
- Specify rules of conduct and consequences. Then enforce the rules fairly.

Keep in mind that research does not show or prove that in-school suspension, out-of-school suspension, or expulsion, make violent students less violent. In addition, there is little proof that ability grouping enhances student achievement. Alternative educators recommend that these practices be discontinued if currently in use.

Now let's dialogue with some school-choice teachers. The teachers interviewed had the following comments about working with students in school-choice programs. These interviews were conducted between September and December 2006.

> Alternative students have a great need for intimacy, yet we place them in huge impersonal schools. They need the right to make their own decisions, yet we place them in environments emphasizing rote learning. There is a large variability among students and within themselves, yet we put them in classrooms where we ignore the need for flexibility. The school I teach in focuses equally on the needs and characteristics of the students. The school is a community of adults and youth embedded in networks of support and responsibility that enhance learning. (American Indian male, 18 years teaching experience)
>
> The best features of my school help students to be active, acquire an in-depth learning, receive a strong support system, teach appreciation of diversity, and foster relationships with the family and the community. (white female, 20 years teaching special education)
>
> Alternative learners must be actively engaged in constructing his or her meaning of the relationship to learning if academic success is to take place. (Hispanic male, 15 years of teaching)

> The students I am dealing with are at risk and do not know how to thrive or survive in a traditional school. They put up walls and refuse to learn. My students do not have the hopes and dreams that inspire academic success. We can no longer ignore out-of-school lives. My school is an integral part of the lives of the families and the students. (African American male, 13 years of teaching)
>
> I spent 35 years of teaching in large impersonal school systems and never once was allowed to do my own thing to motivate kids. Even in my coaching, I had my hands tied by the powers that reside above. Since I joined an alternative school I can teach kids who need me, team teach, do flexible scheduling, and share in the management of the school. (white male, 38 years teaching experience)

Students interviewed during this same time frame said that one of the main reasons for using the school-choice option were the teachers in the school:

> My teacher tells me what is out there to learn, is enthusiastic, and turns me loose to learn at my own pace.
>
> The teachers here are "da bomb." They really care, are sensitive to who I am, and respect me. They are a big part of my life.
>
> I like teachers who teach until we get it. They won't let me fall behind or fail. They make an effort to find out about me . . . where I am coming from.
>
> You are more than just a teacher and principal. You are a friend and someone who is always there for me. I trust you. You make me feel important. You taught me that my mistakes are simply learning experiences. You believe in me no matter what.

All of the teachers interviewed said that they chose to work in school-choice programs because they were allowed to focus on the students. These teachers believe that every child will learn because children rise to the level of expectations that are held for them. They are establishing relationships of love and respect. They offer extra help and tailor the classroom instruction to the child's learning styles and needs. All children need to learn the same basic material, but they won't learn it the same way.

These teachers agreed that there is a need to assess a child's basic needs. Many children who live in poverty come to school each day unable to focus because they are worried about what they will eat for dinner, where they will sleep that evening, and who they will find at home when they leave school for the day. Before we can help students learn, we have to address these most basic issues.

Teachers in school-choice programs love every child, believe that they can and will learn, and never write a child off based on past performance. These teachers ask what is in the best interest of the child and hold all students accountable to the same high standards, regardless of their culture or socioeconomic status. These teachers also hold parents accountable. We can't force parents to help educate their children, but if we give them the tools and the encouragement they need, we can help them begin. Students are assessed frequently, and there is no promotion of students who can't do the work. These teachers realize that the students having difficulty will get farther and farther behind and will help create alternative individualized plans for those who are behind and also for those who are ahead.

The teachers interviewed were in agreement that the one-size-fits-all approach allows too many students to fall through the cracks. We must therefore structure opportunities into each learner's daily schedule that will enable him or her to experience feelings of competence (evidence of test scores, academic success), belonging (valued members of the school), usefulness (made a contribution through cooperative learning and service learning), potency (feeling empowered), and optimism (I can do it).

As teachers, we can honor our students' search for what they believe gives meaning and integrity to their lives and how they can connect to what is most precious to them. We can allow students the freedom to choose what to study and have a say in how they might prove to their teacher that they are making progress. How the content is taught is equally as important as the content itself when we determine mastery. Simply helping the learner discover that knowledge contributes to power, friendship, and fun.

When you ask students to describe their favorite teacher, you most often hear statements like he or she cares for me, wants to help me, and tries to understand me. Students want to be with teachers who create caring interpersonal relationships with them, listen to them, and help them with their problems. Nowhere are these types of teachers needed more than in alternative educational settings, where students often need a teacher who believes in their ability to succeed. Students' personal needs interact with their academic and vocational needs and impact their success in school.

Know the value of "hooking" your students, making the subjects real, and giving your students a reason to learn. Don't let your students ask, "Why do I have to learn this?" Make everything that they learn relate to the real world. Reinforce learning across disciplines and celebrate diversity.

Learning is possible when children look hopefully and joyfully to the future. Unless we project hope for our students, our efforts to teach them to read, write, and calculate won't make a profound difference. A teacher's task is not only to engage students' imagination but also to convince them that they are people of worth who can do something meaningful with their lives.

STUDENTS

> I have developed a passion and determination to keep on learning, to explore the world and to change it. There's something in me now that keeps me excited and my mind going all the time. I feel empowered and free because I can do anything if I try hard enough. (10th grade student)
>
> Am I understanding this? Have I learned anything? If I don't learn anything, then I've wasted my time.(10th grade student)

Here are two students on opposite ends of the spectrum. Both are in classrooms, both are products of school-choice options.

The American educational system is touted as being one of the best in the world. For many people it is the best. However, for approximately 1 million students each year, it is untenable. Some drop out of school, others stay in school but perform well below their ability level and become "in-school" dropouts. Where do they go? What do they do? Do we even care? Thankfully, the answer is yes. The rapid rise in the number of charter schools and alternative schools, as well as other school-choice options, is proof of this.

Students today have enormous talents, ingenuity, energy, and creativity. They have everything it takes to make it! At the same time, many students face incredible barriers to learning. They demonstrate poor attendance, are often tardy to class, cause disruptions and disturbances, are suspended, and are even expelled. They fail to accumulate enough credits to move on to the next grade, and drop out in large numbers as soon as they become of age. Students in school-choice option programs may include young people from troubled families; children who are angry and alienated, bright and bored; and most of all, young people who feel lost or frustrated in large impersonal schools.

Many students are in very poor educational shape, a situation caused by problems they brought in with them through the kindergarten door. This includes poverty, physical and emotional abuse, lack of health care, difficult family conditions, and violent neighborhoods.

School-choice options offer classrooms where students are enthusiastic and absorbed in activities, take time to talk to peers, ask advice, and admire each other's work. Projects are interdisciplinary, with many opportunities for hands-on learning. The work is challenging, related to real life, and rich with meaning. Each child is encouraged to get as much education as he or she has the ability to take.

Our challenge, however, is to make a dent in the growing number of unmotivated students who are essentially forced to attend school. Many students come to school for lack of something better to do.

So what can we do to motivate students? Look at the following two classrooms: Imagine two seventh grade math classrooms side by side. In one, the students are lethargic. Some are staring out windows. The teacher writes an algebraic formula on the board and tries to explain it to the bored class. One girl checks her watch, willing the minute hand to move faster.

In the second classroom, the students are engaged in a lively discussion about whether one of the students can ever save enough money from his part-time job for a new DVD player. Does he have to increase his hours? That changes one part of the equation. Could he find a cheaper device? That changes another part of the equation. The students work on the problem, while the teacher walks around the classroom giving hints and correcting mistakes.

The difference between the two classrooms is obvious. In the second one, the students are given a relevant, real-life problem to solve as an incentive to learn, while in the first, the students are being force-fed a dry formula that bears no relationship to their lives.

"When I think of all the crap I learned in high school" go the words to Paul Simon's classic song of the sixties. This is as relevant to today's students as it was years ago. We can identify with the problem and move on to create an educational program intense and relevant enough to turn a student's life completely around. Teachers must be willing to address the complex social-emotional, academic, and vocational needs of students who choose alternative educational settings. Teachers must be prepared to use novelty, humor, dramas, art, technology, and feedback in their teachings to address the diverse, intensive needs of their students.

How can we reverse a student's years of academic indifference and low expectations for success? How can we build a student's resiliency and transform a student's attitude toward self, family, and community through educational interventions? How do we engage the hearts and minds of our students and unlock the door to their souls? Students are best served in families, communities, and schools that are characterized by caring, high expectations, support, and valued participation. Schooling does make a huge difference in students' lives.

We also need to look at the changing face of racial isolation among our students. Since 1980, 8 million immigrants have arrived in the United States, bringing 2 million students into the nation's schools. These newcomers have changed American schools from biracial to multiracial, multicultural, and multilingual institutions. While the percentage of non-Hispanic white students has dropped significantly, both the percentage and ethnic diversity of nonwhite students have increased. The percentage of black students has remained steady but Hispanic and Asian students have increased. Inside the major cities, the racial and ethnic composition of schoolchildren changed even more significantly.

Magnet schools, alternative schools, and charter schools tend to absorb many of these students because they feel more comfortable in smaller schools with more flexible programs. Children whose native language is not English have also chosen to be placed in language-segregated environments as opposed to mainstream classes that have little or no special language instruction.

The temper of our youth has become more restless, more critical, and more challenging. Added to the challenges of moving through adolescence in a time of great cultural stress are the increasing numbers of both low-income children and immigrant arrivals, creating new and more formidable tasks for the country and its educators.

Overall, school-choice options allow each student to choose to participate in the learning alternatives of his or her school. Students are responsible for their own learning, including attendance, work completion, and timelines for completion. Each student participates in reviewing and shaping their learning environment and the activities of the school. Each student feels that he or she belongs.

Students tell me that they feel the way they learn is recognized and accommodated. Many students develop a personalized plan for success that they review on a regular basis with guidance from staff. Students also feel they are personally informed about credits earned, goals completed, and graduation progression. Most of all, students in these alternative programs experience success in his or her learning on a regular basis. Finally, students tell me that even discipline is viewed as a means of self-improvement and learning acceptable behavior.

Despite the feelings mentioned by the above students, too many children still are not prepared to meet the challenges they face in today's complicated world. Preparing youth requires giving them an effective education. The three traditional Rs (reading, riting, and rithmetic) are just the beginning. What is missing is the fourth R, relevant skills. These skills, including communication, decision making, and goal setting must be part of all students' basic education in order to cultivate motivated, goal-oriented, and community-minded individuals. When students learn the fourth R, there is no limit to what they can achieve. The school-choice programs mentioned in this book focus on these Rs.

Alternative educational programs have increased student achievement by providing the students with the opportunity to become *the best that they can be*. These schools empower students to become independent, respectful, and productive members of their communities. Students are truly given the chance to achieve to her or his fullest potential.

Students always say it best. The following comments were made by alternative students from various programs. They are proud of what they said and asked that their names be used.

Cory: "The teachers help me and correct me without making me feel ashamed or stupid. I will succeed."

Sherice: "Alternative schools help you get an education while you help yourself grow."
Cortez: "I get a chance to show my talents. You give me a chance to prove myself."
Darnell: "You gave me a second chance. I've learned a lesson about responsibility and will handle my business after I leave here."
Quanee: "I don't fit in anyplace but here. This school helps me focus."
Antasia: "All I need to learn is an assignment, pen and paper, maybe a little explaining, and I'm on my way."
Ali Jama: "I appreciate all you've done for me."
Ebony: "I have to work to support my family. You let me leave early to get to my job and still keep up with my homework."
Elijah: "Alternative schools are tight because of the teachers. They care about me inside and outside of the school."
Aries: "I can have an opinion without getting into trouble."
Wia: "I learned to accept myself for who I am."

The young people quoted above are firmly on the path to becoming contributing members of society. They have great potential, great energy, and great dreams. They represent our nation's most valuable resource. Their lives, with all their wonderful possibilities, are the fruits of educating the human will.

FAMILIES

One parent told me about recalling memories of herself as a child trying to make sense of a world full of contrasts and confusions. As a child, she experienced school as a place to put in time. There were so many things she wanted to know and so few occasions in school to learn them. There were explorations to begin, wonders to analyze, discrepancies to resolve, but she felt that school was not the place she could do this.

This parent wants her child to not simply "put in time" but to invest time and effort in solving problems he sees as relevant, problems he wants to solve. The parent feels the traditional school she attended cannot accomplish this for her son. She wants school choice. She wants to find alternative schools that can help her son succeed.

Not only good teachers but also good parents help a child succeed. When parents are interested in and involved in education, they communicate that interest to their children. I have noticed that children whose parents help them at home score higher academically than those whose parents are not involved.

As a parent, you are ground zero in your child's education. Everything you do influences how your child will learn. The following are suggestions from concerned parents:

- Read, read, and read. Read to your child and with your child and openly encourage them to read by themselves.
- Oversee homework.
- Welcome children into adult conversations. Challenge them to think at higher levels and to develop their own opinions.
- Be visible at the school of your choice. Spend time there. Volunteer in the classroom. You can volunteer as an arts instructor, career consultant, coach, computer aide, field trip host, library assistant, tutor, support person for math and reading, and so forth.
- Become mentors, helping students gain the skills and self-esteem necessary to create positive futures for themselves. Mentors can act as role models, coaches, and advisers.
- Meet with your child's teachers on a regular basis, no matter what grade level.

The tension between families and the schools they attend is increasing partly because children in general are not doing well in our country. This is especially true in terms of their intellectual, social, emotional, and moral development. Parents and teachers appear to be lost, confused, and scared, and so are often at odds with each other. We have issues with authority. Our values have changed. The things parents wanted from their children 50 years ago were compliance and cooperation. Now parents want their children to be independent, to question policies, and to form their own perspectives.

Parents need to be brought into the educational community whenever possible. Parents and teachers need to join forces and form working partnerships. Both need to know the difference between words that demoralize and those that give courage, between words that trigger confrontation and those that invite cooperation; between the words that make it impossible for a child to think or concentrate and the words that free the natural desire to learn.

Never before have so many young people been exposed to so many images of casual cruelty. Never before have they witnessed so many vivid demonstrations of problems being solved by beatings, bullets, or bombs. Never before has there been an urgent need to provide our children with a living model of how differences can be resolved with honest and respectful communication. Teachers and parents can give the students protection against their own violent impulses. When the inevitable moments of frustration and rage occur, instead of reaching for a weapon, help them reach for words they've heard from the most important people in their lives.

Remember that there is a direct connection between how students feel and how they behave. When children feel right, they will act right. Accept their feeling. Family support and healthy family relationships are correlated with student success. However, maintaining family relationships can be a challenge. Many families have become weary of the behavioral and/or academic difficulties that have characterized their child's experience with the school system.

Schools cannot meet the challenges of reform without first communicating with the parents. The process of bringing parents together, talking, listening, developing a shared vision, and creating a plan of action has value in and of itself. It brings parents into conversation and decision making. It builds trust and good will.

Parents will speak out forcefully if given the chance. When asked what they really want from schools, the parents interviewed said they wanted a curriculum that promotes cultural competence and appreciates diversity and instructional methods that promote cooperation, interaction, and success for all students. They also want public conversation that is sensitive to the perception and values of the community as assessment practices that include alternative methods that allow for cultural differences.

What do parents want from teachers? Most parents said that they want to identify how well teachers know and care about teaching and care about their children, and they want communication that is open and honest. They want teachers to share stories, their high expectations and goals for their children, and how parents can reinforce learning at home. Parents want to see the classrooms in action.

Parents are trusting schools with the well-being of their children. Schools must take that responsibility seriously. If educators show parents that they honestly care about their children, parents will be more inclined to place faith in the educational system and accept its role in the life of their child.

One parent said, "I do not want to sacrifice my child on the altar of the future. Talk to me about today." Another said, "I want teachers to be accessible, responsive, and cooperative."

Many parents do not realize that the educational world has changed dramatically since they were in school. Even through rose-colored glasses, we knew that school was no picnic and was far from perfect. Because our public school system has deteriorated, parents, teachers, and other individuals have taken it upon themselves to find alternatives to the traditional system. It is important for parents to know that they have alternatives to the neighborhood schools.

How do parents know it is time to look for another educational approach for their child? Here are some of the signs:

- Does your child hate school? Children are natural learners. If your child says he hates school, listen.
- Does your child come home from school bored and cranky? This is a sign that the educational experiences are not energizing but debilitating.
- Does your child come home complaining about conflicts he has had in school or talking about unfair situations he has been exposed to? This is a sign that the school does not have a process for conflict resolution, and communication is lacking.
- Has your child stopped reading for fun or writing for pleasure? This is a sign that these activities are not being valued in the classroom.
- Does your child refuse to do homework? This may be a sign that homework is not interesting, does not meet his or her needs, and is extinguishing natural curiosity.
- Does your child refuse to talk about what happened in school? Maybe nothing exciting is taking place.

- Does the school nurse or guidance counselor suggest that your child has some strange three-lettered disease, like ADD (attention deficit disorder)? Have you been told your child needs Ritalin or some other drug? Maybe the school has EDD (education deficit disorder). It is time to remove your child from that situation.

If children have exhibited several of the above characteristics, it is time to start looking for an alternative. Check out school-choice options (charter schools, magnets, private schools, and alternative schools).

Families are fortunate to have a wide variety of choices when they are considering the best schools for their children to attend. When choosing a school, keep in mind there is no one right school for all learners. Each child and family has preferences for the kind of educational environment they want. Figuring out exactly what you want in a school is not a simple task. When you imagine the ideal school for your child, you may picture colorful classrooms, dynamic teachers, and a variety of extracurricular programs. But you need to weigh your child's needs, your family's values, and practical constraints. If you have more than one child, you may want them to attend the same school even if they seem suited for different environments.

The options can be overwhelming. It is important to narrow them down. Consider the location of the school, the child's learning and social needs, the before- and after-school programs, how you would like to be involved in your child's education, and the technology used at the school.

When schools and families team up to help children learn, everyone wins. In Houston, Texas, administrators went to their students' homes and sat on stoops with family members to "cut contracts" with parents, enlisting their help in the effort to reduce school violence. The result is safer schools and steadily rising test scores. In Murfreesboro, Tennessee, schools stay open until 6 p.m. to allow parents to work without worry, knowing their children are involved in constructive activities. In Benton Harbor, Michigan, parents help teachers and administrators by working as classroom aides and office support staff. In New York City, teachers link the classroom to home by operating a telephone homework hotline that students and parents can dial in the evening to get help with assignments.

These are but a few examples of the many ways alternative schools are encouraging greater family involvement in education. They're discovering that school-family partnerships are an important way to help children learn and a great way for schools and families to help each other.

However, schools and families still remain disconnected in too many communities. Schools of choice are now making an effort to involve parents in decision making, helping teachers reach out to parents, making parents feel welcome, overcoming language barriers, using technology to link parents to the classroom, and encouraging school-family partnerships. These schools are reaching out to parents and listening to what parents have to say.

Alternative schools are schools that fit families. One complaint families have with traditional schools is that the schedules of the schools and families are a bad fit. Schools still expect families to adjust to the schools' routine and that makes it very difficult for most families. Alternative schools realize that accommodating the constraints faced by families would be better for children's lives in general and for their education.

As we have seen, given the changes in the American family over the last several decades, a school which is organized around an agrarian calendar and the assumption that a mother is waiting at home, does not mesh with the reality of modern urban America.

In many alternative schools, the school building is opened early in the morning and not closed until evening. Breakfast and snacks are provided, volunteers coordinate athletic programs, tutoring programs are in place, and clubs and special interest organizations are sponsored by community involvement. In some cases the school building also serves as the location or offices of the welfare department, health clinics, or legal aid.

You have heard the phrases *knowledge is power* or *equality begins with education*. Parents need to take charge of their child's education. Learning isn't over when the last bell rings. Support and encourage and celebrate academic success. Salute your children for doing right. Promote pride. Parents need to be vigilant, know what is going on in school, be informed, know what your child is learning, be involved, be vocal, and be visible, making sure the school knows who you are.

We live in a world that is constantly changing; yet we still are introduced to educational practices that were developed a century ago. As parents, if we want to have maximum impact on our children, if we want to prepare them for the world they will inherit, we have to adapt to our changing world. As parents we have to experiment, take risks, even be willing to make mistakes as long as every decision we make is in the best interest of our children. Children will not learn from adults who don't love and care for them.

When schools encourage parents to get involved, grades improve, test scores and graduation rates rise, absenteeism falls, and expectations for students soar. The achievement gains are greatest for those students who are farthest behind. Parental involvement can and does take many forms in schools across this country. We see parents involved on site teams, on advisory councils, in creating charter schools, in the classrooms, and in PTAs. The amount of involvement varies greatly, but parental satisfaction in the education that their children receive seems to increase. Parents feel empowered.

Education is about teaching our children to find pleasure in learning. Children need adults to care for them in addition to their parents. They need someone at school who knows them well. Parents also need a personal relationship with the school.

Alternative learning environments reflect the needs of the students, the teachers, and the parents. The student becomes the center of teaching and learning. The needs of the student relative to personal, social, emotional, behavioral, basic learning, and career and talent development are carefully considered. The focus is on establishing student success and responsibility for personal learning. The school climate motivates learning. Teachers directly influence students, and students work hard to succeed if engaged and challenged. Once parents and teachers see how well students are doing and how much everyone enjoys school, parents, teachers, and students become partners in the learning process and are the educational environments biggest supporters.

As Martin Luther King Jr. once said, "Developing intelligence plus character, that is the goal of true education." Parents, teachers, and students must work together to achieve this goal.

11

THE FUTURE OF EDUCATIONAL CHOICE: DOES IT WORK?

> Education should alter the lenses through which one sees the world. Education can provide a point of view from which what is can be seen clearly, what was as a living present, and what will be as filled with possibility.
>
> —Unknown

We have arrived at an important turning point in American education. With the dawn of a new information age, knowledge has become our greatest strategic resource and learning has become our greatest strategic skill. Until recently, many Americans could lead productive, satisfying lives without a college degree. Now, for all of our people, the indispensable key to unlocking the American dream is a good education and the ability, motivation, and confidence to learn throughout a lifetime. We simply cannot leave anyone behind.

Young people in school today have passed the baby boomers to become the largest generation in history. Yet our nation will thrive in the 21st century only if we make sure that their education surpasses the education we received from the generation before us. As student enrollment grows and an aging teaching force retires, will we be able to attract, train, and retain the million new high-quality teachers needed in the next 10 years? Will we make sure every child can learn in a safe, modern classroom? Will we set high academic standards and provide the intensive support and accountability needed to help our children meet them?

We must boost student achievement for all children and close the academic performance gap between children of color and white children. Our mission should demonstrate that people of all racial and ethnic backgrounds can not only live and work together, but can also enrich and enable themselves and others and build our nation's future together. We must provide all of our people with a quality education if we are to achieve our mission. We must dedicate ourselves along with our communities to help every child realize his or her promise. We can no longer afford to ignore or even linger while we consider this challenge.

Our school system is filled with paradoxes. We claim we want every child to learn, but we promote children to the next grade level even when they haven't mastered the skills that they should. We claim we want every child to learn, but we do not hold teachers and administrators accountable for student achievement. We claim we want academic achievement from our students but we place teachers in schools based on seniority rather than merit.

I have found many schools that are focused on the morale and welfare of adults rather than on the academic, social, and emotional needs of the children. Why, when we know it costs more to teach children who are chronically below academic standards, do we spend the same amount of money to educate every child?

We must realize that we cannot reach all children with a traditional curriculum. Therefore, we should start diversifying our curriculum to meet *all* students' needs. This means that we must stop embracing the status quo and start embracing change. We need to stop serving children out of a sense of duty and start educating children out of a sense of love. Children do not learn from adults who do not love them.

We must hold schools accountable and develop clear plans, goals, and objectives and use strategies to establish student success. We must hold teachers accountable for improving student performance and establish child-centered classrooms where actual teaching takes place. We must hold parents accountable to read with their children, check and monitor homework, and establish communication with the schools.

We must make school more exciting than the streets. Education should be about how to make a life, which is quite different from how to make a living.

Instead of drafting national academic standards and implementing impersonal one-size-fits-all teaching methods, allow parents, teachers, students, and communities to work together to design schools that address student needs and interests. Emphasize respect for parents, teachers, and students. Allow for personalized instruction, active learning, and the development of the capacity for astute, probing thought.

Living in the midst of rapid change, most of us have had a hard time truly seeing the essential features of change. But if we are to understand our students and determine what kinds of schools will be most helpful to them, we must first consider how a changing world is shaping today's young people and their future.

There are four broad categories to consider: work, learning, citizenship, and motivation for learning. Work requires skills to survive in a technological age. Learning is what is needed to survive in the "information age." Citizenship includes critical thinking, political and civic engagement, and civility. Motivation for learning includes respect for authority as well as considering the impact of a consumer-driven economy.

Throughout the ages, communities and cultures have had to decide what is most important for the young to know and be able to do. In earlier times, issues of survival and transmission of traditional culture and beliefs were the main preoccupation. Many answers about what children needed to know were self-evident. Elders taught the young what their elders had taught them.

Now, in an era of information glut and rapid change, we must think very carefully about what we want all children to know, as well as how we can access their expertise. We must reconsider what it means to be an educated adult in the 21st century.

Alternative education for alienated students is seen as the response to a global problem, that the system of public education is failing to meet the challenge of demographic and social change, and children are unprepared for the workplace. Provisions to meet the needs of these students have frequently developed out of community initiatives, which may or may not be effective.

We must ask ourselves: what do effective, worthwhile programs look like? The answers are in front of us:

- The teachers know their students well.
- The curriculum is intellectually challenging and engaging.
- Student voices are heard.
- Real world learning is taking place.
- Students are provided with an emotional "support system."
- Close ties with families are forged.
- The environment is safe and respectful.
- Economic and social needs (poverty, unemployment, health care, homelessness, criminal activity, drug abuse, family breakdown, and teenage pregnancy) are addressed.

Alternative programs are based on the tenet that different individuals learn in different ways and that there is no single best approach to education. These programs provide a greater responsiveness to a perceived educational need within the community. This means including a more focused instructional program, a shared sense of purpose, a student-centered philosophy, a noncompetitive environment, greater autonomy, and a more personalized relationship between students and staff. Remember that children are unique in their educational needs. The main hallmark of quality in alternative programs is individuality. Strategies to maintain student attendance and behavior management are also a piece of the foundation. Poor attendance and inappropriate behaviors are major barriers to student learning that must be overcome.

Quality programs invest in teachers as resources. The relationship between teacher and student is high priority as is sensitivity to cultural differences.

Assessment of student performance is also an essential component of quality programs. Too often, assessment is viewed as being separate from teaching. Yet quality assessment can give teachers the knowledge to better instruct their students, which will lead to increased student academic growth. However, too much assessment diminishes the positive educational impact of assessment. A balance between too little and too much assessment must be reached if we are to meet the instructional needs of the students. This balance is important for students in alternative educational environments because many have serious instructional needs and teachers must plan for unique presentation of material. Assessment should ultimately be utilized to improve teaching and learning.

Successful school innovation is also about time: making time, taking time, and finding more useful ways to spend time. We must build in time for teacher collaboration and for high-quality professional development, which should be driven by school goals and student performance data.

Schools of choice as covered in the previous chapters coordinate curriculum with state standards and are willing to undergo careful scrutiny to ensure this has been done. These schools also use outside resources, especially parents and community members to implement their programs.

If we are truly interested in choice, we need to focus on programs such as improved teacher training, ongoing staff development, smaller classes, multicultural curricula, and adequate resources for all children in all schools. We must also address the problems affecting our urban communities including poverty, unemployment, low wages, and inadequate health care.

It is not that our society doesn't know how to teach our children, but that we do so unequally. It is not that we don't have successful schools, but that they are clustered in affluent neighborhoods. It is not that we refuse to spend money on children, but that it is disproportionately spent on the already privileged. The central issue facing American education is how we, as a society, choose to resolve these inequalities and provide choices so that all children attend quality schools and receive a quality education.

Money matters. It is a prerequisite for reform. It is immoral and unjust that our urban and rural schools tend to receive far fewer resources, even though they confront far more complicated problems. School choice is an answer for these issues.

How do we get out of this educational quagmire that we find ourselves in? I invite readers to join me in stripping away all the historical accidents that surround questions of American education today, and begin with a fresh view of family, education, and ourselves as if we were in a pure state of nature. One of the reasons we have such difficulty in achieving rationality and justice in education is because our discussions begin as if, whatever else happens, out first obligation is to preserve the essence of the status quo. We end up captives of and tampering with a destructive system instead of replacing it. We are in a mess and we have to fight through a great maze before we can even think clearly. Our vision is blurred by long habit, an inertia manipulated by vested interests tied to political power.

Seen from a fresh vantage point the natural ends and objectives of educational policy will be quite clear. In a democratic society such as our own, those natural ends begin with the welfare of the individual. We want the best assurance we can get that the individual capacities of all citizens within society will be developed to the largest extent possible. We hope that the educational system will help produce individuals able to work effectively within the contemporary economy and particularly within the conditions of a highly competitive international economic order. We need to visualize alternative approaches to the achievement of those objectives.

We must also avoid one of the biggest errors that schools make today. They try to exert too much control over the lives of the students. It is critical that children be allowed to develop in ways that are consistent with their own unique personalities. The system must conform to the needs of its students not vice versa. The child must know that he is in charge of his own life and future. Children are people. They can develop confidence in themselves as learners, find answers for themselves, and prepare for life-long learning. I believe that school choice and alternative education can be a way of restructuring education.

Americans are free to make decisions about their health, education, and welfare. We can choose what to eat, how to exercise, whom to marry, where to worship, and which candidate deserves our vote. But most Americans have little ability to choose how or where their children will be educated during their most critical formative years.

The government decides where the vast majority of children in this country attend elementary through high school, and the fate of most children is determined by their address. Parents seeking the best schools must either pay private tuition on top of the taxes they pay to support the public schools, or pay a premium to move to a neighborhood with good public schools. A lot of children do well under this system of choice, but many do not. The children hurt the most are those whose families cannot afford an alternative to the public school in their neighborhood.

In an advanced information-age economy, lifetime earning prospects depend on the quality of education more than ever before. It should be no surprise that school choice has recently enjoyed growing support among parents and the general public. Public school choice allows parents to send their children to alternative schools and, for those who can afford it, to private schools.

Many forms of school choice have been subjected to rigorous academic study, and the results are simple. School choice works. Students' test scores are higher and school spending and taxes are lower. The Hudson Institute's national survey of charter schools revealed that students who were failing at their previous schools performed average or better in charter schools. A state-funded voucher program in Milwaukee showed low-income students performed better in math and reading than those who did not receive vouchers. The same was true in Cleveland, New York City, and San Antonio. Homeschooled students scored higher on standardized tests than either public or privately schooled students and their scores increase more rapidly as they progress from one grade to the next.

Parents want school choice. Surveys consistently show that parents whose children participate in school-choice programs are much more satisfied with their chosen schools. Cleveland parents whose children received vouchers expressed much more satisfaction with their chosen schools' academic quality, safety, discipline, and attention paid to their children than parents whose children were still in public schools. Surveys of low-income applicants for privately funded scholarships in Washington, D.C. and Dayton, Ohio, agree.

School-choice programs typically have many more families interested in participating than can be accommodated. Such excess demand reveals that many parents are well-informed and concerned about their children's education, and they want options for their children other than their assigned public schools.

The argument for school choice is not just that choice improves academic achievement, but also that choice accommodates parents' views about the type of education that they want for their children. The extensive Catholic school system in the United States, for example, was established largely because poor Catholic immigrants feared that public schools would indoctrinate their children in Protestantism. In present-day America, educational choice would put an end to seemingly endless arguments over sex education, textbook choice, and censorship in school libraries. Parents could simply choose schools that reflect their values instead of fighting to impose their values on their neighbor's children. The result would be an immeasurable but long-overdue increase in civility and social harmony.

What will education look like 10 years from today? Will it be a delivery system or a system of management as well, emphasizing many alternatives and school-choice options?

Schools of choice offer hope to the institution of public education by providing community support, positive results, and an ongoing effort to innovate, improve, and disseminate their success. These schools require vigilance regarding the needs of each and every student. Students choose to participate as do staff.

Schools of choice work with the community, giving students the tools they need to be successful in whatever areas they choose. They adapt curriculum and schedules to students' realities. The entire school environment is used to maintain success, not just one or two classes. The attitudes of staff and faculty are sometimes as influential on youth as their home environments. These schools also utilize a blend of diverse instructional practices that complement individual student needs, interests, and learning styles. Most of all, the schools of choice mentioned in this book demonstrate a willingness to experiment, thus staying on the cutting edge of educational issues and change.

We must work together as families and educators. Eric Trist once said, "No one can force change on anyone else. It has to be experienced. Unless we invent ways where paradigm shifts can be experienced by large numbers of people then change will remain myth." Do not allow school choice to become another educational myth.

All over America, parents are opting for something other than the standardized public school offerings, often at great effort or expense. The choices they are making, whether it be charter schools, private schools, alternative schools, or homeschooling, are for learning communities that offer an environment where both teachers and learners are empowered and where innovation and flexibility are common practices.

These schools are found in crumbling inner-city buildings, in strip malls, in old rural school buildings, and in newly converted warehouses. They have optimistic sounding names like Capstone, Crossroads, and Learning Enterprise. These alternative learning environments are popping up all over the landscape, mainly in urban areas but also in suburban and rural areas.

Schools of choice are addressing at-risk students who are discouraged learners, those who, for whatever reason, do not achieve in the standard elementary or high school program. Poor attendance, habitual truancy, academic gaps, and teenage parenthood also plague many students today.

American economic leaders have identified the characteristics they value in the workplace as oral and written communication skills, problem-solving ability, self-management capacity, and a cooperative working style. The factory model schools so prevalent in the United States do not produce those outcomes.

Homeschooling of school-age children has expanded during the past several years. Self-help groups have sprung up to assist parents who choose to educate their children at home.

Private schools have always existed in America at all levels of education, but public moneys have never supported them. There are lobby groups active in the legislatures that have renewed efforts to approve voucher systems for use in private schools.

Charter schools continue to grow. Independent for-profit corporations such as the Edison Project and Education Alternatives, Inc. have made some inroads in the management of schools. Alternative high schools are tackling the dropout issue. They are also providing services for gifted students and students having problems with a single class and meeting students' specific needs. Many programs are competency based with portfolios and demonstrations required and personal growth valued.

The learning community formed in alternative schools of choice is the key to academic success. Common-bond learning communities can be the central idea around which can be developed the complex balance of environment and forces needed to meet the needs of today's and tomorrow's emerging generations.

The problem with the traditional system is that nothing has been done to assess why students impede their own learning and success as well as that of other students. We must realize that students are people first, people who need respect, trust, support, and simple human courtesy. In the past, students were restricted to traditional public school agendas. Instructional delivery methods were used which required students to receive a daily schedule of disconnected curriculum in a time frame that did not recognize student differences.

Why don't we get the message? Why don't we understand? Why don't educators realize that school-choice options are implementing school-improvement initiatives as the basis for providing an effective teaching and learning environment? Smaller schools, personalized learning, shared decision making, a respect for student learning styles, and community involvement through service learning and social service at the school site are cogent.

There is nothing wrong with alternatives. They are a major way to recognize that all children are individuals with different learning styles, preferences, and needs. The best school-choice systems will offer educational alternatives to everyone, regardless of class, race, gender, or at-risk status. Such systems celebrate diversity. By focusing on educational ideals and ideas, erasing politics from the equation, and concentrating on the child, those concerned with children and youth would inevitably come to the realization that a variety of educational alternatives is a significant way to meet the academic needs of most students.

The dominant forces in education continue to sing from a sheet of music that is both out-of-date and out of tune. We do not need more tests, more standardization, and larger, impersonal schools.

The fact is that these approaches do not work, and all of us with a stake in America's children can't afford to keep singing the same old song.

There are many across the country who are working toward a better education for our children. All kinds of people: parents, teachers, principals, policy makers, employers, and countless others. They embrace the vision of school choice.

When I think of school choice, I see places of adventure, magic, and excitement. I see an atmosphere of celebration that will make coming to school a privilege rather than a chore. These schools are physically and emotionally safe places to express and share feelings and ideas, to create, and to enjoy. These schools are places where the human spirit will be nurtured and given a chance to grow, where courage will be modeled and rewarded. The students are learning to appreciate diversity and not scapegoat and persecute those who are not quite like them. Most of all, these schools are helping students become aware of the enormous range of their human potential. This then leads the students to form visions of what can be and then to acquire the understanding and skill to make their visions come true.

We are still a nation at risk, but it is our children and their future that are more at risk than our economy or national security. Many students who go to American public schools today are very much at risk, especially low-income and culturally diverse children. They are at risk of graduating without the skills needed today for work, life-long learning, citizenship, health, and personal growth. They are at risk of leaving high school without once experiencing the joy of learning or connecting with a caring adult. They are at risk because their lives are all too often lacking in purpose or direction, meaning, and hope. And with so many of our children at risk in these ways, our future as a nation is also at risk. These children are our future. We have no other.

We must create alternative schools, schools you may choose, that inspire both hearts and minds. We know what they look like, how they work, how they can be held accountable, and how much better the results are for all the students who attend these schools. We also know that, by becoming a focus for community action, they enrich the lives of many adults as well. Our children are counting on us to make the right choices.

What will the world be like for tomorrow's children? When I look at my 18-month-old grandson's face, bright with wide-eyed curiosity and joyful expectation of love of life, I see wonderful possibilities. But when I look at the challenges he and his generation will inherit, I see that these possibilities will not be realized unless today and tomorrow's children learn to live in more environmentally conscious, equitable, and peaceful ways.

Today, young people often feel powerless to change the course of their lives, much less the course of the world around them. Many become immersed in the me-firstism and overmaterialism that permeate much of our mass culture. They are futilely seeking meaning and belonging in the latest fad or commercial offering. Some bury their pain and anger in drugs, alcohol, gangs, and other destructive activities, unconscious and seemingly uncaring of the effect their actions have on themselves and others. Many become violent, under the thrall of hate mongering or religious fanaticism, or simply because our video games, television, ads, and movies make violence seem normal and even fun. It appears that the vast majority, including our young people who expect to get a decent job or go on to college to pursue a professional career, fail to see how what we do with our lives is both affected by, and affects, our cultural beliefs and social institutions.

There are many factors that contribute to all of this. But there is one factor that can play a major role in providing young people with the understandings and skills to both live successful lives and create a more sustainable, less violent, more equitable future: education.

The schools of choice mentioned in the preceding chapters can help young people meet the unprecedented challenges of a world in which technology can either destroy us or free us to actualize our unique human capacities for creativity, caring, and life-long learning.

If enough of us are committed to personal and collective transformation, if together we keep moving forward, as Marian Wright Edelman wrote, "putting one foot ahead of the other, basking in the beauty of our children, in the chance to serve and engage in a struggle for a purpose higher than ourselves" (1996, p. 37) we will succeed in laying the educational foundations for a safer, more livable, more loving world for all children and the generations still to come.

Deborah Meier (2006), (educational reformer, writer, activist, and considered the founder of small schools) advocates for today's children when she says, "Since kids have this huge range of different needs, different interests, and different ways of learning, we've got to have a wide diversity of schools."

I repeat, give our students and their families choices regarding education.

It is said that the Masai warriors in Africa greet one another with the words, "Eserian Nakera." The lyrical phrase means "and how are the children?" The traditional response is "all the children are well."

American education will be complete when the schools embrace that Masai saying in word and deed. It goes hand in hand with the saying, "It takes an entire village to raise a child." All of this is just fluency rhetoric unless we make it real.

It is our duty to make certain that our children get the high-quality education they need and deserve. Then, we, the villagers of America, can rightfully say, "All the children are well."

REFERENCES

Barker, T. (2001). *Opposing view points*. Seattle: University of Washington Press.

Barr, R., & Parrett, W. (1995). *Making a difference*. Thousand Oaks, CA: Corwin Press.

Barr, R., & Parrett, W. (2001). *Hope fulfilled for at-risk and violent youth: K–12 programs that work*. Needham Heights, MA: Allyn and Bacon.

Bickler, E. (2005, January/February). Homeschooling: Is it for you? *Home Education Magazine.* Retrieved December 12, 2004, from www.home-education.org.UK.

Carnegie Foundation for the Advancement of Teaching. (2004). *School CHOICE*. Princeton, NJ: (ED 352 727).

Costen, S. (2005, February 13). Parents see values in a private school. *Richmond Times-Dispatch*, p. 1.

Edelman, M. W. (1996). *Guide my feet: Prayers and meditations on loving and working for children.* New York: HarperCollins.

Education Week (2006, June 11). *2006 Annual Survey.*

Friedman, M. (1955). Choice, chance, and the personal distribution of income. *Journal of Political Economy, 61* (4), 277–290.

Heritage Foundation. (1998, July/August). A nation still at risk. *Policy Review.*

Hill, P., Foster, G., & Gendler, T. (1990). *High schools with character.* Santa Monica, CA: RAND (ED 327 597).

Home Education Network/UK. www.home-education.org.UK/.

Jencks, C. (1966). *The academic revolution*. Cambridge, MA: Harvard University Press.

Kelp, J. (1997, January/February). Becoming unschoolers. *Home Education Magazine*.

Lilliard, P. (1972). *Montessori: A modern approach*. New York: Schocken Books.

Meier, D. (2006, November 4). Speech at the Coalition of Essential Schools Fall Forum, Chicago, IL.

National Center for Educational Statistics (NCES). (2005, May). *Private schools: A brief portrait*. Washington, DC: U.S. Department of Educational Publishing.

National Home Education Network (NHEN). www.NHEN.org.

National Home Education Research Report. (2000). Washington, DC: U.S. Department of Education.

Natriello, G., McDill, E., & Pallas, A. (1990). *Schooling disadvantaged children: Racing against catastrophe*. New York: Teachers College Press.

Oakes, J. (1985). *Keeping track*. New Haven, CT: Yale University Press.

Raywid, M. (1989). *Alternative schools*. Bloomington, IN: Meyer Stone Books.

Steel, L. & Levine, R. (2004). *Educational innovation in multiracial contexts: The growth of magnet schools in American education*. Washington, DC: U.S. Department of Education.

U.S. Department of Education. (1974). *Let magnets guide the way*. Washington, DC: Office of Educational Research and Improvement.

U.S. Department of Education. (2005). *Private school enrollment continues to climb*. Washington, DC: National Center for Educational Statistics.

Wehlage, G. & Rutter, R. (1987). *Dropping out*. New York: Teachers College Press.

Williams, M. (2004). *Opposing viewpoints: Education*. San Diego, CA: Greenhaven Press.

Witte, J. (2004, December). *Milwaukee parental choice program*. Madison, WI: University of Wisconsin Institute of Public Affairs.

Woolf, V. (1929). *A room of one's own*. London: Harcourt, Brace, and Jovanovich.

Yancey, D. (1995). *Schools*. San Diego, CA: Lucent Books.

Young, T. (1990). *Public alternative education*. New York: Teachers College Press.